P
SKYROCKET L

Michael is the best trainer we've ever had work with our teachers and leaders.

Kole Knueppel
Director, Center for Transformational Educational Leadership
University of Notre Dame, South Bend, Indiana

I have had the opportunity to work with Sonbert in a number of contexts and am always impressed by his ability to quickly diagnose classrooms and provide exactly the right professional development to support teachers and leaders to improve instruction. His Skyrocket model puts those same tools he intuitively uses into the hands of educators to support instruction.

Ryan Scallon
Assistant superintendent, The School District of Philadelphia
Philadelphia, Pennsylvania

I am elated and grateful for my Skyrocket experiences. Skyrocket is passionate about equipping school leaders with what they need to lead. The practical, easy, and fun-filled conversation enhanced our coaching sessions. My leaders can't stop talking about things that they have learned through Skyrocket. We will Skyrocket!

Janel Hawkins
Senior director of school transformation, Milwaukee public schools
Milwaukee, Wisconsin

The framework is so clear that it allows us to find the biggest levers for our struggling teachers and our more advanced teachers.

Antonio Vance
Executive director, Great Oaks Charter Schools
New York City, New York

Skyrocket has provided our principals, assistant principals, coordinators, and instructional coaches the ability to impact teachers because of the specific feedback we are able to give. I have participated in the trainings with the coordinators and instructional coaches, and we always end our trainings on fire for more learning. It has been the most impactful training for our district.

LaCreasha Stille
Assistant superintendent of curriculum, Gainesville Independent School District
Gainesville, Texas

Michael's training combined the necessary headlines and overarching concepts in a compact crash-course that helped individuals understand how to effectively implement and fit existing structures for observation and coaching.

Michael Nguyen
Senior managing director, teacher leadership development
Teach for America

What I love about Skyrocket leader coaching is that I see the concepts that were delivered at training being implemented at our schools immediately thereafter. It is practical, best-practice skills that are instantly applicable and impactful.

Robert Rauh
Chief education officer, Milwaukee College Prep School
Milwaukee, Wisconsin

Skyrocket provides high-leverage feedback and action steps to yield fast results, true to its name. In fewer than eight months of collaboration, we've made double-digit growth in culture and climate, measured by teacher and student data. The real-time, in-the-moment coaching has transformed my leadership and, in turn, impacted teacher effectiveness. The best professional development experience of my career!

Kellie Porter
Principal, Russell Byers Charter School
Philadelphia, Pennsylvania

Skyrocket helped to transform instructional coaching at our school. The framework provides teachers with clear, high-impact action items for them to focus on. The model gave our faculty a powerful list of agreed-upon expectations that will quickly improve instruction. It encourages our coaches to be more data-driven and direct in working with our teachers, and to not shy away from directly coaching and practicing instructional strategies during coaching meetings. The model is direct and easily gets teacher buy-in. We saw the quality of instruction in both our new and returning teachers improve dramatically using the model. Skyrocket was truly a school-changing program for us.

Tim Gallo
Principal, St. Thomas the Apostle School
Chicago, Illinois

By using Skyrocket, I have observed teachers developing their practice rapidly, which led to an increase in student achievement on benchmarks and exit tickets, as well as state assessments. The team at Skyrocket is changing the game by solving real-world school problems.

Rashaun Reid
Principal, KIPP Vision Academy
Atlanta, Georgia

The Skyrocket coaching framework has had such a positive impact on my leaders and teachers! The frameworks are straight to the point, the manual inspires creative coaching, and I can see the impact in my classrooms. In addition, the Skyrocket team has been super supportive every step of the way!

Joanna Hightower
CEO, Alliance for Progress Charter School
Philadelphia, Pennsylvania

Michael's analysis is spot on—I admire his multilayered approach (principals, coaches, teachers, and students) and how he models the appropriate techniques. His strength of relationships allows him instant credibility and access to our teams.

Michael Gaal
Former K8 network leader, Education Achievement Authority of Michigan
Detroit, Michigan

Michael's support has been invaluable for helping us set a high bar in terms of the expectations of both adults and students as we pursue rapid growth in student outcomes. The Skyrocket rubric is highly praised and well used by our coaches because it breaks down supporting teachers into specific and actionable steps.

Lauren Vargas
Director of instructional coaching, EdConnective

The Skyrocket framework is both practical and usable. Its simplicity unmasks the elements of effective teaching that often get lost in feedback and evaluations—our teachers know exactly what skill they are working on, get meaningful practice with that skill, and apply it immediately in the classroom. The results are unmistakable.

Matthew Glass
Academic coaching manager, American Paradigm Schools
Philadelphia, Pennsylvania

By the winter to spring assessment window, our ELA growth was over 132 percent and math growth was 111 percent on the MAP Assessment across our eleven schools.

Ryan Krienke
Director of schools, Seton Catholic Schools
Milwaukee, Wisconsin

Michael has helped me transform the way I lead a school. In addition to working with him to effectively problem solve the challenges that school leaders regularly encounter, Michael has worked with me to create the systems and tools necessary to lead in a way that is proactive and ensures strong student outcomes in a positive school climate.

Stephen Janczewski
Principal, St. Malachy School
Philadelphia, Pennsylvania

Michael Sonbert is a rare breed in education today. He provides a universal, clear-cut, no-nonsense leadership and coaching approach that motivates educators to want to make and then plan for shifting their paradigm—for the betterment of all school stakeholders. His teachings are transformational, encouraging, collaborative, and insanely on point.

Sean Deiters
Principal, Countryside Academy
Benton Harbor, Michigan

Working with Michael Sonbert and Skyrocket has changed the type of leader I am. I was a strong teacher but at best a mediocre leader. Working with Michael and the Skyrocket framework taught me that what brought me success in the classroom when I was *doing* all the work is not what would bring me success as a leader of others.

Julie Pickhaver
Principal, St. Frances Cabrini
Philadelphia, Pennsylvania

We saw a 15 percent growth for seventh- and eighth-grade math and 13 percent growth in sixth-grade ELA on the New York state exam. Sixty-five percent of our sixth-grade students hit their math MAP goals as well.

Atiyah Harmon
Principal, Great Oaks Charter Schools
New York City, New York

Skyrocket's Leader Academy was a powerful opportunity to unpack, explore, and put into practice the most critical actions leaders in education can take to strengthen outcomes for students. The sessions were designed to directly and immediately impact my practice and provided me new professional energy.

Nicole Schmidt
Senior director of teaching and learning, LUMIN Schools
Milwaukee, Wisconsin

Adoption of the Skyrocket model has been transformational for our school leaders and our teachers.

Mark Ketterhagen
Principal, Milwaukee College Prep School
Milwaukee, Wisconsin

Our teachers are learning the best strategies that lead to academic growth.

Rich Jensen
Chief academic officer, Agora Cyber Charter School

The Skyrocket Leader Academy is a game changer for the principals and deans in our network. The leadership framework is like a roadmap to running a high-quality, high-achieving school.

Paul Hohl
Director of schools, Seton Catholic Schools
Milwaukee, Wisconsin

SKYROCKET YOUR TEACHER COACHING

SKYROCKET YOUR TEACHER COACHING

How Every School Leader
Can Become a Coaching Superstar

MICHAEL CARY SONBERT

Skyrocket Your Teacher Coaching:
How Every School Leader Can Become a Coaching Superstar
©2020 Michael Cary Sonbert

All rights reserved. No part of this publication may be reproduced in any form or by any electronic or mechanical means, including information storage and retrieval systems, without permission in writing by the publisher, except by a reviewer who may quote brief passages in a review. For information regarding permission, contact the publisher at books@daveburgessconsulting.com.

This book is available at special discounts when purchased in quantity for use educational purposes or as premiums, promotions, or fundraisers. For inquiries and details, contact the publisher at books@daveburgessconsulting.com.

Published by Dave Burgess Consulting, Inc.
San Diego, CA
DaveBurgessConsulting.com

Library of Congress Control Number: 2019956616
Paperback ISBN: 978-1-951600-04-4
Ebook ISBN: 978-1-951600-05-1

Cover and interior design by Melissa Jane Barrett

For Max, Teddy, and Penny
You've taught me the most important things I know.
Including that indescribable love exists.
Run full speed toward your dreams, and please do
good and have fun at every stop along the way.
Love, Dad

CONTENTS

Foreword — xii
Introduction — xiv

PART ONE: The Skyrocket Approach
1. Big Ideas — 2
2. Expertise Is Everything — 8
3. The Framework — 15

PART TWO: Ignition
4. Sound Bites — 24
5. Collecting Data — 28
6. Strand-Specific Data — 32

PART THREE: Launch
7. Preparation — 40
8. Communication — 50
9. Accountability — 64
10. Twenty-Two-Minute Meeting Execution — 69

PART FOUR: Orbit
11. Real-Time Coaching (RTC) Mindset   82
12. Real-Time Coaching Techniques   89

PART FIVE: Landing
13. Best Practices   98
14. Common Questions   105

About the Author   113
Acknowledgments   114

FOREWORD

Frederick M. Hess

Michael Sonbert is a hard-ass. You should know this before you buy his book.

If you're looking for the usual upbeat, jargon-laden, happy talk about coaching and school improvement, you'll want to look elsewhere. In my experience, most professional development and instructional coaching makes it all sound so easy. If you think the right thoughts, believe this research, use these protocols, and hold regular meetings, you'll see wondrous results.

Michael Sonbert calls BS on all of this. After all, these approaches rarely deliver the promised results.

Sonbert believes, I think rightly, that it's not all this hoopla that matters, but the discipline, rigor, and precision that you bring to what you do. He wants you to do the hard things—to focus explicitly and precisely on how a teacher engages a student, introduces a concept, or makes sense of why something didn't work.

Like everything else that matters, this sounds easy, is hard to do, and is bloody hard to do well. That's why, for all the time and money spent on preparation, training, PD, PLCs, workshops, instructional coaching, and the rest, most schools don't do this stuff very well.

And that's why I'm writing this foreword. I'm generally a skeptic when it comes to PD and instructional coaching. I don't usually endorse books like this—I'm more likely to ignore them, or to mock them.

But the first time I saw Sonbert in action, in a Milwaukee elementary school, I thought he was onto something important. I've participated in or observed too many post-observation debriefs to count. Whether genial or firm, they're usually a mix of pointers, reflections, and encouragement. Even the good ones tend to feel a little slapdash.

Watching Sonbert conduct a debrief was the opposite of that. There was no one-on-one chatter—the debrief played out in a small, intense but collegial team. Every word was measured. The questions were finely honed. The suggestions precise. The experience, I suspected, was a glimpse into what it would be like to watch Leonard Bernstein mentor a violinist or Bill Belichick explain a defensive technique.

Now, Bernstein or Belichick could coach me all day and I still wouldn't be able to play a lick. So, I'm not promising this book will work miracles. As with anything else of value, it'll depend on whether you're willing, able, and inclined to use it. But if you're sick of the feeling that you've seen plenty of change but little real improvement, this may be the book for you.

A number of years ago, I penned the book *Cage-Busting Leadership*. In it, I encouraged school and system leaders to stop accepting frustrating rules, routines, rhythms, and cultures, and to start changing them.

What Sonbert offers here is one powerful way to help make that change happen. Now, let's be clear: I'm not saying that his Skyrocket approach is the only way—or even necessarily the best way—to do so. But it's a promising one.

Sonbert's emphasis on execution and doing things right should be a beacon in a field where passion, good intentions, and formulaic processes have too often been allowed to excuse ineptitude or sloppiness.

So, if I haven't yet scared you into seeking out a cozier, cuddlier, more familiar alternative text, I'd urge you to read this book. Read it tonight, and take its advice to heart. After all, Michael Sonbert is the best kind of hard-ass, the kind who approaches his work with the passion, precision, and unrelenting discipline that is the hallmark of excellence in any endeavor.

And I think our schools need more of that. A lot more.

Good reading. And good luck.

INTRODUCTION

When I was a new teacher, I had a coach. She was great. Friendly and supportive and knowledgeable. We talked about my lessons and she gave me a lot of ideas to incorporate into my teaching. One piece of coaching she gave me was about the volume of my voice: it was too loud as I was instructing, and it was likely off-putting for the students sitting in front of me. At the time, and in hindsight, she was right. So, I lowered my voice. But it wasn't an earth-shattering shift. It didn't change me as a teacher. It didn't change what my students did or what they produced, even though it *was* helpful.

When I was a more advanced teacher, I had a coach as well. He, too, was equally friendly, supportive, and smart. He shared ideas and materials, and I really enjoyed working with him. He provided me with sentence starters, and as a result, my students started using academic language in response to my questions and their classmates' answers. Again, that was very helpful, but again, this coaching didn't radically change my practice or what my students produced.

I eventually became an instructional coach myself. I wasn't half bad: a solid relationship builder with a strong ELA background and the ability to motivate teachers. Still, if I'm being totally honest, most of what I coached teachers on early in my tenure didn't drastically change their practice. It was what I call "suggestion-based coaching." I thought of something, and I shared it. I shared it in a "Hey, it would be cool if you tried this" type of way. And I have no doubt I made *some* helpful suggestions at the time. Likely my material-share and my support around lesson planning were appreciated. And, I believe my teachers enjoyed working with me. Still, something was missing.

If you're reading this, you likely agree that teachers need to be amazing for students. And we know that, in many places, principals, assistant principals, instructional coaches, lead and master teachers, site-based teacher leaders, and so on, all coach teachers. But, too often, like me or the teachers I coached early on, the teachers aren't improving quickly enough.

The question is, why not?

I eventually became the director of strategic partnerships at Mastery Charter Schools in Philadelphia, and after that, the founder of Skyrocket Educator Training, through which I have trained school leaders and teachers from district, charter, and faith-based schools from over eighty cities around the world, and have provided significant onsite support to leaders and teachers in places like Detroit, New York, Milwaukee, Chicago, Indiana, Delaware, Dallas, and Connecticut, to name a few. Through this work, I have witnessed things like what I described earlier happening in schools and classrooms nearly everywhere: well-meaning and passionate school leaders simply weren't moving their equally well-meaning and passionate teachers nearly as quickly as they needed to. And while, when it comes to instructional coaching gaps, it can seem like every school is different and every challenge is unique to that building and those leaders, teachers, and students, there are really only *three key trends* that are appearing nationally.

The first trend exists in schools where school leaders don't have any grounding documents or shared language around instruction and teacher coaching. There isn't anything they can point to that lays out precisely what excellent teaching or excellent coaching looks like. So, often, after an observation, leaders speak to teachers from a place of what they like or think or feel versus using unbiased data and proven best practices to drive their feedback. Meetings often sound like, "I really like the way you did X. Maybe next time you should try Y." In these schools, there's little to no mention of student data, very little modeling or training, and the feedback is either acted upon or not. Because shared language is lacking, even the most well-intentioned and passionate leaders can't speak succinctly with other leaders about teachers, students, or their progress; and, because teachers aren't clearly being told what to do to be more impactful, some teachers are frustrated. However, most simply have an inflated sense of their skill level and effectiveness. Which makes sense, as their "coaching" meetings are usually very general. The leaders talk a bunch about what they like and make a few suggestions, but they rarely give any actionable next steps. As a result, teachers think they are excelling, when in fact they would benefit from intense training on basic to advanced skills. But the truth is, in many of these schools, observations and feedback rarely happen anyway. These leaders spend most of their days in their offices, responding to emails, organizing field trips, handling operations issues, and meeting with parents. And often, poor instruction is accepted as the norm.

The second trend exists at schools that *do* have certain frameworks or rubrics around teaching and coaching. In many cases, leaders attended trainings on those models, and in other cases, the trainers came to them. The problem here is that these frameworks and rubrics are very dense, and much of the language is gray ("most students, some students"). So, often, the leaders aren't experts at *the very thing* they're attempting to train their teachers on. They have these impressive frameworks, but they're barely being used; when they are being used, they aren't being used effectively. I observe leaders from all around the country speaking very generally and hesitantly about instruction while flipping through multiple-page documents that they themselves haven't fully internalized, and neither have their teachers. Leaders in these schools try to observe teachers and provide meaningful feedback (though the "feedback" often comes in the form of emailed "action steps," which the teachers need to have real training on, rather than just an email about), but it's often *so* broad and across multiple domains, so their meetings aren't as intentional as they can be. Also, teachers can feel totally overwhelmed by the amount of feedback they receive, sometimes being told they need to tighten up their entry routine, write more meaningful objectives, and have students working in groups, all in *one* meeting. I call this "feedback shrapnel." It doesn't make teachers better. They just duck to get out of its way, all while potentially feeling like they're failing miserably because they're getting feedback on *so much at once*. Without leaders and teachers hyperfocused on what good instruction is, without leaders narrowing in on every teacher's most important next step, and without significant training and follow-up *on* those next steps, these docs (which I do believe contain a lot of the "right" stuff) are as useless as the most decadent cheesecake is to a person who is lactose intolerant.

The final trend is around leaders' cherry-picking of skills that aren't the most important next step for their schools. A powerful example of this occurred at a school I visited in Detroit. The leaders had just run a training on Cold Call that they were very excited about. They'd read about Cold Call in a text and decided that it was exactly what their school needed. The problem was, they missed the mark. This *wasn't* the school's most logical next step. Because when I asked teachers in the building if it was an effective training and if they felt like it was what they needed, many responded that they simply wanted to know how to get their students to sit down. I get that no one becomes an educator so they can practice giving directions or designing routines for handing out papers. They get into it so they can ask deep questions and share their passion for their content with young people. So, I get why these leaders defaulted to Cold Call before some of the more foundational classroom culture skills. But in doing so, they risked totally disinvesting their teachers and their students. Think about a teacher who's having trouble building a strong culture in his class, asking a question that no one is listening to, and then cold calling on a student—who likely didn't even hear the question—to respond. I witnessed this. As you can imagine, the more the teacher pushed, the angrier the student got, until eventually he erupted and stormed out of the room. Interactions like this lead teachers to lose faith in their leaders, and students to lose faith in their teachers. And then, in some cases, teachers default to saying toxic things like, "That doesn't work with my kids," when it's time to try executing that skill again.

These trends, and the learning I've acquired from many brilliant educators I've met over the years, led me to create the approach we currently use at Skyrocket. And I wrote this book because I want to share that approach with you. Because I believe it can support you in increasing your effectiveness as an instructional leader. Whether you're a thirty-year veteran principal, charged with training your entire team, or a brand-new master teacher who's coaching one or two teachers, I believe something (hopefully many things) on the following pages will resonate and positively impact your coaching. And the more effective your coaching is, the more effective your teachers are, and in the end, that's great for your students.

I'd like to make one point before you dive in. While some PD and some programs promise quick fixes to really complex issues in schools, Skyrocket is just the opposite. We play for the long game, coaching the leaders with whom we work to shift their thinking and, as a result, their actions. We coach school leaders to adopt the mindset that *execution is everything* in this work, so following our approach halfway will yield halfway results. To use a fitness analogy: Some groups are like the new fad diet that promises you'll lose weight if you eat only tree bark and sleep upside down for two weeks, while we're the personal trainer who gets you out of bed every morning at 5 a.m. and gets you on the treadmill for an hour of interval training.

That being said, you may not be ready for that level of intensity. Maybe your school is just dipping its toes into the world of instructional coaching. Maybe you're a master teacher who teaches most of the day, but you coach one teacher a couple of times a week. Maybe you work at a school, network, or district that has a robust coaching program, but the approach is much less direct and precise than ours, and you don't feel comfortable marching into the superintendent's office, demanding she adopt our approach. Or maybe you're still getting your coaching legs under you and you need a little more time to build up the confidence to coach as intensely as we're prescribing. I want you to know that *all* of these things are okay. Yes, we want people to coach intensely and to make radical change in schools. We also want people who do have barriers to think creatively about how they can still execute at a high level. But even if you can't go *all-in* just yet, for whatever reason, I still believe you'll get a lot out of this book. Whether it's around collecting data more effectively, or noticing and addressing low-bar language, or defining criteria for the teacher you're coaching, I'm confident you'll increase your effectiveness, even if you execute on 10, 20, or 50 percent of what's described on the following pages. Because even fifteen minutes on the treadmill is way better than eating tree bark and sleeping upside down.

PART ONE:
THE SKYROCKET APPROACH

1
BIG IDEAS

We are what we repeatedly do.
Excellence, then, is not an act, but a habit.
—Aristotle

Imagine you decide, after years of wanting to learn how to play the piano, to hire a piano teacher and begin lessons. You start slowly, one key at a time, following your teacher's lead. She hits a note. Then you hit the same one. She does it again. So do you. Soon you're playing the easiest of all piano songs, "Chopsticks." You're slow, but you're getting it, building confidence along the way. You're thinking, I can do this. I'm playing piano. And then your teacher looks at you and says, "Now let's work on some Tchaikovsky."

Likely, this would shock you. Or frustrate you. Confuse, anger, or disinvest you. If your teacher told you to play Tchaikovsky without first modeling what it looks like to play Tchaikovsky at a high level, that would likely disinvest you further. If her feedback felt random, not specific enough, or not actionable, or if it was absent altogether, you might want to give up. You might even think, I'll tolerate the time I spend with this person, but really, I can't wait for them to leave so I can go back to doing things my own way.

Here's the thing: it's just not possible to become proficient at "Chopsticks" and Tchaikovsky at the same time, the same way it's not possible to become proficient at giving clear directions and checking for understanding at the same time. It's too much, and these tasks are too different.

This is why the *core belief* behind the Skyrocket approach is that *teachers should be coached where they are and not where you want them to be*. That can be a challenge for school leaders who feel the urgency to "fix" everything at once, and it's going to be a theme throughout this book.

Our approach is a long-game approach. It's about building foundational skills, and layering on top of them more and more advanced skills. This means no more training a teacher on writing objectives when they can't get their students to stop talking, because even the most effective lesson, in the hands of a teacher who can't get students' attention, will fall flat. Also, the teacher will likely feel disheartened and may lose faith in their coach and, potentially, the students. A coach in this situation might even start to doubt themselves. And lower coach confidence often results in less directive and more general coaching—the same type of suggestion-based coaching I provided to teachers early in my career.

Coaching teachers where they are does not mean we lower the bar. Certainly not. In fact, I'd argue Skyrocket is one of the most—if not the most—intense coaching models in education today, and the intensity and precision of our model will become evident as you read on. We train school leaders to land on a teacher's highest-lever teacher action to increase student outcomes. After that, the leader designs and executes a practice session that will move the teacher forward immediately. Then the leader provides real-time coaching and follow-up support to ensure the teacher action sticks. (This three-step process—Ignition, Launch, and Orbit—has ample time dedicated to it in this book.)

If you have designs on running a marathon, I wouldn't train you by having you run an entire marathon on your first day. We'd have to build to that. That might be your end goal, but trying to do that on day one or in week one would be a formula for failure, just like asking the first-week piano student to play "Chopsticks" and Tchaikovsky in the same lesson. Without adequate support, success is even more difficult. That's why leaders often find themselves having the same conversations with teachers in March that they were having in September. It's too hard to provide feedback on, collect data on, or design practice for too many skills at once.

I was in a school recently that had a schoolwide initiative around higher-order questioning. This seems like a reasonable thing for a school to be working on. We want students to engage with harder and harder material, and higher-order questioning is a great way to help get there. But as I began sitting in on coaching meetings and talking to teachers, many were so far away from being able to create the space for a higher-order question to even land with their students that it was largely a waste of time to provide them training on it. I shared this data and the school leaders agreed. They then decided to coach only a *few* teachers on higher-order questioning (as it was a logical next step for them), while coaching everyone else exactly where they were.

What I'm suggesting is that, even if a schoolwide instructional focus is present, individual teachers are still coached—in the *finite* amount of time a coach has with a teacher—on the skill *they personally* need to work on to most increase student outcomes in their room.

Right now, you may be thinking, how do we land on *that* thing? And how do we train on it? How do we ensure the teacher gets good and stays good at it? Our three-step process provides the answers for these three questions. But before we get there, I want to reiterate that core belief: *Teachers should be coached where they are and not where you want them to be.* Because to get them to where you want them to be, you need them to get really good where they are now.

Now that we've discussed this core distinction in our approach, I think it's important to make another distinction, between what *we* at Skyrocket consider coaching and what many schools, networks, districts, and consultants consider coaching. What most people in education consider *coaching* is what *we* consider *support*. It's important to name this, because you're likely reading this and reflecting on your own teacher development program, which is great. But I'd like to ask you to think about coaching and support in the following ways throughout this book: for the sake of uniformity, for the sake of clarity, and for the sake of simplicity.

Support, as we see it, is discussing a lesson, maybe sharing some materials, or talking about a student discipline issue. It's a *conversation* about the teacher's class. It's not terribly structured, no skill is modeled, no practice occurs, and there aren't any deadlines or deliverables set at the end of it. It's talking about how to get James to stop sleeping in class. It's helping a teacher organize a lunch meeting with some students he's struggling to build relationships with. It's telling a teacher to use popsicle sticks to ensure more students are called on (this one happens *a lot*). It's showing the teacher the worksheet you used when you taught main idea and telling them that they can use it too. And meetings like that are *fine* sometimes. But those meetings likely don't *build skill*. And what was discussed likely isn't transferrable (like a deep dive into writing objectives would be, for example). When a meeting like that ends, even if the teacher feels great, he probably didn't get *better* at anything. He might have a few more tools in his toolbox, and he likely feels supported (hence the name), but he's not more well-equipped to design tomorrow's lesson or to deliver clear directions. That's because those things that were worked on are prescriptions and *not* habits.

This distinction between prescriptions and habits is important. A prescription is a basketball coach telling her star player, after the player suffered an Achilles injury, to switch to a new brand of sneakers because that brand offers more support in the Achilles area. This is helpful and important, but it's not a habit. It happens once and it's over. Like an instructional leader suggesting a teacher switch the seats of two students who are talking to each other throughout instruction.

Coaching, as we see it, is very different. It's structured and focused. It's heavy on modeling, practice, design, and feedback. It's directive and grounded in data. All in service of building habits that teachers will continue long after the coaching cycle is complete.

I opened the introduction of this book writing about my first and second coaches. I didn't, however, mention my third coach. My relationship with her was *very* different. In her first observation of me, I closed the lesson by telling twenty-eight middle-school students that they'd mastered the objective (I knew to do this much). But when pushed by her, after the students left, to name *how I knew* that they'd mastered it, I couldn't provide anything beyond, "I just know my students."

This wasn't good enough for her (thank goodness). Because while I was doing a lot of student-to-student responses, group work, and peer editing, I wasn't always planning effectively. Which made modeling and then providing feedback to students that much harder, as I didn't totally know what I was looking for. And if success was somewhat of a mystery to me, it was *definitely* a mystery to my students.

My coach trained me to provide a model and a clear set of steps for every lesson, as well as an evaluation rubric I could use (which became a self-evaluation rubric that *students* could use), to determine if they'd *actually* mastered the day's content.

I never taught another lesson without providing and then modeling a transferable set of steps for students (my class didn't become less interactive, however, but *more*, as students were now engaging more deeply and providing more robust and precise feedback to each other when asked, because they more clearly knew what success looked like). Using these steps, I was able to more effectively check for understanding, as I knew *exactly* what I was looking for. Her coaching led to *radical* change in my practice and what my students produced. And while there are many measures of success (and, yes, students are much, much more than test scores), that year, 35 percent *more* of my students scored proficient or advanced than their citywide peers on the state assessment. And the next year, 43 percent more did.

As you think about this distinction between support and coaching, I'll ask you to think about the following questions our coaches ask themselves after *every* coaching meeting they have:

- Did that teacher just get significantly better at something?

- Do they know their next steps?

- Have I put systems in place to hold them accountable?

If the answer to any of these questions is no, we know the meeting could have been more impactful.

As you read on, and as you reflect on your own teacher development program, I invite you to consider those questions as well. My hope is that if you currently have a *no* for any of the three, that you'll have a *yes* for each one by the end of this book.

2

EXPERTISE IS EVERYTHING

*I'm so much more gratified by my life
now that I have an expertise.*
—Angela Duckworth

*People who have expertise just love to
share it. That's human nature.*
—David Baldacci

If you are committed to driving the instructional vision of your school, it's immensely important that you *are* and are *seen as* an expert. Teaching is the hardest job in the world. It's like trying to file papers while falling out of an airplane. And while I'm sure being a brain surgeon is hard as well, I'm pretty certain that as the brain surgeon is about to make the first incision in the patient's head, nobody calls out, "Can I go to the bathroom?!"

Teachers are absurdly busy, managing a dozen things at once, so making sure that your feedback to them is precise and accurate is of the utmost importance. Otherwise, you risk disinvesting the very people charged with educating the students.

I'm fortunate enough to get to observe, speak with, and spend time with teachers all over the country. They're different in so many ways. Some teach every subject. Some teach one. Some teach students who come up to their knees and others teach students who tower over them. Some are the only teacher of their grade and subject in a small school. Others are one of a half-dozen who teach that grade and subject in a school with north of 1,000 students.

What they often have in common though, is this: many don't see their bosses—meaning principals, assistant principals, deans of instruction, etc.—as a value-add when it comes to what's happening in their classrooms. And often, they don't respect the instructional expertise of the person who's leading their schools.

Put more simply: teachers don't think their bosses know what they're talking about.

This is damning. And it's happening all over the place.

To be clear, teachers sometimes like their bosses. They often say they're nice and supportive, but when it comes to seeing their bosses as experts who drive the instructional vision of their schools, they rarely view them as such.

To know why, I'd like to take you on a brief journey into the past, to the first of my two jobs washing dishes and sweeping floors at Italian restaurants on Long Island. My boss was as nice and as friendly as they come. But he'd casually stroll in around dinner time and have the bartender pour him a glass of red wine. He'd sit at the bar, drinking his wine and eating the day's specialty, even as the evening rush picked up. When customers had issues, he dodged them, often leaving it to less-senior members to handle. On one occasion, when the pizzamaker was out sick, the boss left *me* to make pizzas for the day. But I'd never done this before and he'd never taught me how to do it (despite telling me for weeks that he would), so my "pizzas" were misshapen, undercooked, and, I'd imagine, pretty gross to eat. He'd show up late, change the menu last-minute without reason, and pay us when it was convenient for him, but certainly not on a regular schedule. And on the rare occasions when he'd come into the kitchen, all I could think was, "Get out of here. You're in the way. You don't know what we do every day. So leave us alone so we can do our work."

The way I felt about this boss is what many teachers express about their school leaders. They express the opinion that they're successful (to whatever degree they *are* successful) not *because* of the school leader and their support, but *in spite* of them. In spite of their misaligned feedback. In spite of their cancelled meetings. In spite of their disconnect to the content. In spite of their unhelpful PD. In spite of their lack of follow-up. In spite of their infrequent visits to their classrooms.

This makes sense when you think about what happens at a typical school. The school year begins in the summer with some in-service training, usually around school and classroom norms, school culture, and content. Sometimes there's goal setting and a revisiting of school values, with time to set up classrooms mixed in. Then students come, and in a lot of ways, teachers are then on their own. Even in schools with a lot of teacher coaching, where school leaders see each teacher every week for meetings and observations, teachers are still doing most of their work alone. And that's in a school where the level of coaching is *high*. In most schools it's *significantly less* than this. I recently had a teacher tell me, in March, that her principal hadn't observed her all year. While most leaders see their teachers more often than this, for teachers, even an average amount of visits can feel really infrequent. Think about this: if a school leader is observing every teacher in her building nine times per year, which is once a month from September through May, and that teacher teaches four blocks of math a day, that means that teacher is teaching 720 blocks of math a year (four blocks multiplied by 180 days of school), 711 of which she's teaching without feedback or direct coaching.

The point is, teachers are used to doing things on their own. Even in schools where support is sky-high, where a school leader does fifty or seventy-five observations a year per teacher, teachers still do the overwhelming majority of their work solo.

So, what often happens is teachers begin to see their school leaders as nuisances. As people totally out of touch with what's *actually* happening in classrooms. This is why some teachers push back on evaluations (or want them eliminated altogether). Because it can feel like the person evaluating them doesn't know what they're doing. Leaders pick up on this, but they're often not sure how to address it. So, they default to doing two things: hiding and high-fiving.

First, they spend a lot of time "hiding" in their offices. People like to feel successful, and school leaders are no different. They can feel the icy stares from teachers when they enter their rooms. They can see their feedback isn't being implemented. So, they sit in their offices, responding to emails, meeting with parents, handling operations issues, and in some cases, spending the entire day with a student who's gotten into trouble. These leaders are not visible throughout the day, choosing small victories with a handful of parents and students at the expense of positively impacting the larger school community.

Other school leaders decide to pull back from anything instructional at all. They know their feedback isn't valued. They can feel that they're in the teachers' way. So, they become cheerleaders for the school. They circulate the building, patting people on the back, checking in to make sure people are okay, and "high-fiving" everyone they see, all the while, handing over the instructional reins to teachers. These leaders are usually liked by their teachers, which is what they're striving for. But almost no one takes them seriously when it comes to impacting student outcomes.

In some of our trainings, we ask school leaders to write a job description for themselves. Not what they *actually do* every day, but what they believe they *should do* every day. Their answers are surprisingly aligned. They *usually* write something like this: "To positively impact students by coaching and supporting teachers." But so many aren't doing this. They're either hiding or high-fiving.

To clarify, handling operations issues and meeting with parents are important parts of a school leader's job. And a leader who has strong relationships and celebrates teachers is a great thing. What I'm suggesting is that doing *only* these things, out of lack of confidence or to simply avoid the pressure and inevitable discomfort of being the instructional lead in the building is (a) not an effective way to move the instructional needle for teachers and students and (b) not what *leaders themselves* report they should be doing.

Something else often happens, and it happens whether the school leader is hiding *or* hive-fiving. Some school leaders try to "fix" their instructional (and overall leadership) misses by implementing something new in their schools. They think this *new thing* will be the change the school has been looking for. The change it desperately needs. It could be a new math curriculum or a new approach to school culture. It could be a shift to blended learning or new SMART Boards. And on and on. All these new things do is lead to disinvestment and reform fatigue from teachers who likely don't believe the school leader will be able to support the execution of whatever the new thing is anyway. Think back to my example of the boss at the Italian restaurant. It wouldn't have mattered if he upgraded every ingredient in the building so that we used only the finest ingredients found anywhere. And it wouldn't have mattered if he overhauled the entire menu from top to bottom. Building renovations, new job titles, and even changing the name of the restaurant wouldn't have mattered. *He* was the issue. No *new thing* was going to fix that.

And while many leaders will point to the same culprit—lack of time—as the reason for their instructional misses and ineffectiveness, this is almost *never* the case. Yes, time is in short supply in this work (I'll talk more about time later on). But it's the hiding and high-fiving that are stopping them from being extraordinary leaders for teachers and students.

But we can fix that.

The solution is for a school leader to be an expert. An expert who provides accurate feedback, delivered succinctly, with clear criteria for improvement, followed by concrete goals and next steps. An expert in the way Tom Brady is an expert at throwing a football or Simone Biles is an expert at the balance beam.

Let's journey back into the past again to my other job at an Italian restaurant. This boss was a hothead. He screamed. A lot. He threw garlic knots at us when we messed up. He cursed at us. But here's the thing: I liked working for him. When a customer had an issue, he was front and center to handle it (sometimes throwing garlic knots at them if he thought their concern was petty). When the head chef called in sick, he stepped up and spent the night cooking and sweating with us in the kitchen. When it snowed and one of the delivery drivers got stuck in a snowbank, he was out there with us, in knee-deep snow, pushing the car out. He was there first and left last. He was an expert at every part of the business. He knew how to do everything, was willing to do *anything*, and he watched every staff member and critiqued us continually. He'd even give me feedback on the size of the balls of dough that would eventually become pizzas, which I was sometimes charged with rolling. If there was one that was too small, even slightly, he always caught it. And while I didn't enjoy being yelled at by him (and I don't suggest doing this with your teachers, ever), it was *always* after I'd done something that didn't meet the bar he'd set for us. It was always in an attempt to make me better.

While it's likely not possible for any school leader to be an expert at everything from phonics to chemistry and from abstract art to *The Scarlet Letter* (and I'd argue they shouldn't be), it *is* possible for you to become an expert at building classroom culture, lesson design and delivery, and deeply engaging students, regardless of content. But to do this, you need a simplified approach that allows you to simultaneously build your knowledge, capacity, and confidence. And I dive into this approach in the next chapter.

But there's *something else* you need as well. And for some of you, this will be a *major* mindset shift. But without adopting this mindset, you simply won't be able to access this book to the same degree as someone who has this mindset. Without adopting this mindset, you won't be nearly as effective an instructional leader as you possibly can be.

Ready? Here it is: You need to be okay with naming that the students in your school are *your students*.

This seems obvious, but too often school leaders tell teachers things like, "You know your kids better than anyone," and "You know what's best for your students." Whether this is true or not is not the point. The point is, *all* the students in your school are *your students* first. And last. Yes, their teachers spend the most time with them. But you're the one who's ultimately responsible for their success (or failure). You're the one sitting in data meetings with your bosses and stakeholders while teachers are off on summer vacation.

You're the one looking at a sea of red, being grilled by your superintendent, or members of the archdiocese, or your board, about how you're going to turn it all to green. You're the one whose picture makes it to the newspaper when test scores drop. You're the one parents, neighbors, and reporters want to speak to when they have an issue. The buck stops with you. Even if you're an instructional coach and not the principal or AP, I'll bet you're still held more accountable for student results than teachers are.

Here's the point. You *must* own that the students in your building are yours so you can feel confident giving feedback, asking teachers to shift course, interjecting in lessons, and running professional development. This is nothing against your amazing and talented teachers, but you need to stop signaling to them that *they're* the ultimate authority on what's best for the students, when *you're the one* who's ultimately held accountable for what those students produce. It'd be like a restaurant owner telling her head chef that she can put whatever she wants on the menu because she's in the kitchen the most. Okay, but then what happens if only *some* of her dishes are delicious? What if customers start complaining? What if the food critic from the local paper is coming in tonight? This restaurant owner has undermined herself and made it exponentially more difficult to provide feedback to the chef because she's given her own power away.

It's on you to lead the charge. It's on you to provide direction. It's on you to adopt this mindset so you can be an unstoppable force for change in your buildings.

3
THE FRAMEWORK

Simplicity makes me happy.
—Alicia Keys

I designed the Skyrocket framework to provide both a North Star for the school leader looking for more direction and a lifeline for the school leader drowning in documents and verbiage. If you are planning on continuing to use the framework you currently have while adopting our approaches to communication, data collection, practice, etc., I still suggest you read this chapter. It will provide valuable rationale for the design of the model, and it may support you in clarifying some of the outcomes and action steps in the framework you're currently using. You can find a free download of the Skyrocket Framework for Teacher Coaching and Evaluation here: http://www.wewillskyrocket.com/frameworks/.

Our framework is a simple, one-page document (front and back), because you don't have a lot of time. It's short, like this book, because you *need* short. Your teachers need short. I *was* a teacher who tossed his instructional guidebook into a drawer in August and didn't look at it again until I was cleaning out my room in June. But all over the country, *teachers* have the Skyrocket framework taped around their rooms so they can refer to it. Because it's simple. Because it's short.

The framework is made up of three strands, and it's hierarchical. If you have success stories of teachers radically improving at both designing entry routines and at having students respond to each other using academic language simultaneously, please email me. I'd love to come see it. But for now, I consider those stories to be the education equivalent of yetis or chupacabras. They *may* exist, but if they do, I'd think we'd have more evidence by now.

Each strand within the framework has between seven and thirteen teacher actions. Likely, these teacher actions are familiar to you. I did not pull them out of thin air. They're amalgams of the actions you'll see in some leading education texts, notes from thousands of teacher observations, evidence-based best practices, and my own work as a teacher and instructional coach at Mastery Charter Schools. They're the *most important* actions that will increase student outcomes. You'll notice things like teachers using timers and shaking students' hands as they enter the classroom are absent. This is intentional as those things, while potentially helpful (or not), don't definitively increase students being on task (the Strand One student outcome), whereas, getting students' attention with a countdown or call-back signal, does. You'll notice that in each strand, the teacher actions progress from planning and design to execution.

On the bottom of each strand is a rubric for evaluation. This can be used by school leaders who don't have another tool for teacher evaluation, or by those who do, but who find our framework more accessible. However, some school leaders either don't do evaluations, or they have a framework they're mandated to use to do them. That's fine, as this rubric can still be used to gauge progress as you're coaching the teacher. There's also a rubric-free version on our website for the school leaders who think that simply seeing a percentage and words like "unsatisfactory" or "developing" will cause teachers to shut down.

As a side note, many schools use Skyrocket for coaching while also using something entirely different for evaluations. Often because they're mandated to use that other framework. This is totally fine, as our model works well paired with the Danielson Framework, the TNTP Core Rubric, and the state-created frameworks that are often used to evaluate teachers. And, in fact, we've seen some leaders in this position be able to *increase* buy-in around coaching amongst staff. This makes sense, as the concern about coaching also being evaluative is eliminated because a different framework is used for each.

Strand One is classroom culture. The student outcome goal is for students to be on task. And while this can be defined on a really granular level (and certainly, do this at your schools if you'd like—many school teams have), broadly, it's defined as students following directions. Here, you will coach teachers to create a structured and warm environment where systems are in place, expectations are both high and clear, and students feel supported. Class routines have been predetermined and teacher directions are easily understood. You'll coach teachers here to praise students and express their belief in them throughout, and to redirect students, without sarcasm or negativity, when they don't meet expectations. The class will run like a well-oiled machine.

Strand Two is content mastery. The student outcome goal here is for students to make progress toward mastering the content. Unlike Strand One, where most school leaders and teachers would like 100 percent of students to *always* be on task, in Strand Two, 100 percent of students *always* mastering the content would likely be a flag that the content is too easy. That's why the student outcome is students *making progress* toward mastering the content. I'll write about collecting data shortly, but for now, think of progress as students showing evidence that they understand the concepts, the steps, and what they need to do to master the objective. Their work may not be perfect or totally complete, which is fine. What you're gauging, though, is whether there's evidence they will be able to do it, or at least most of it, and that they're on their way to doing just that. In this strand, teachers are coached to be expert planners who write meaningful objectives for every lesson, for which they then design lesson exemplars and corresponding steps. They introduce the content in a way that engages kids, and then they model the process students need to follow. They check for understanding while both differentiating content and updating students as to their progress toward mastery. Strand Two is still very teacher heavy. This is intentional, to ensure teachers are highly skilled at every piece of lesson design and execution.

I won't spend a lot of time on teaching here, but I do think it's important to specify that, in Strand Two, for teachers to get students to master content, content needs to be presented and teachers need to teach it. This seems obvious, but in my observations of thousands of lessons at over one hundred schools over the past eight years, the biggest trend I've observed around teaching is that teachers often *aren't teaching*. Which isn't to say students aren't doing anything (though sometimes they're not), or that teachers aren't working hard, because, mostly, they are. But frequently, classrooms are missing explicit instruction from teacher to students. Instead, students are working in workbooks or on worksheets. They're on laptops or working on review packets. Sometimes it's a project that they're working on in groups or pairs. Other times they're "following along" as the teacher reads from a novel, and then answering some questions afterward. But when these teachers are asked by me or by their school leaders "What skill are you teaching to students today?" overwhelmingly, these teachers can't name one. They often share what students are *working on* but are less able to name the transferable skill and process the students have been *taught*. Of course, this isn't on teachers, but rather on leaders who haven't trained teachers to do this. Or who have, but haven't held them accountable for consistently and intentionally teaching, every period, every day. Either way, if, as you're reflecting on your own school, you're realizing that many of your teachers aren't teaching a transferable skill every day, you'll need to shift this before you can coach them around planning and lesson delivery. As I said to a group of Chicago principals recently, who were asking how to most effectively gauge student progress toward content mastery: "When you enter a classroom, you should not be like a person hacking her way through the Amazon rainforest with a machete, trying to see two feet in front of her. What students are working on, and the process they're following, should be very clear from the moment you enter."

Strand Three is rigor. Our rigor strand is designed to shift the cognitive load onto students. However, the teacher still needs to have an expertly planned lesson with objectives, steps, higher-order questions, and activities meant to push student thinking. The student outcome is the percentage of students deeply engaging with content throughout the lesson. This goes beyond students writing down the day's objective or sharing a few things they remember from yesterday's lesson. It goes beyond calculation, listing, and identifying, and requires students to make predictions, comparisons, and to analyze text. Whereas a Strand Two teacher might ask students to copy the day's objective in preparation for the lesson, the Strand Three teacher might put an exemplar response on the board and ask students to write down what *they believe* the day's objective is based on their analysis of this exemplar response (though the teacher would ultimately share what the actual objective is). Or maybe, based on that exemplar response, they would be asked to come up with their own set of steps to reach content mastery (again, there would still be a correct way or multiple correct ways to do this, as determined by the teacher). In this strand, the teacher doesn't tell students whether they're right nearly as much as she engages students in peer-to-peer collaboration, discussion, and debate so that they can productively struggle with material and grapple with others' ideas.

I should mention here that rigor is my *least* favorite word in education. Not because I believe that designing and executing rigorous lessons isn't important or beneficial for students—because obviously I do, as we have an entire strand dedicated to it—but because I see "rigor" as an education buzzword, often used by educators who, when pushed to clearly define rigor, struggle to describe it in any measurable way. Oftentimes, however, those same school leaders then land on "lack of rigor" as the reason why their teachers and students are underachieving. This, to me, is a misdiagnosis of what's actually happening in their schools. And this misdiagnosis can lead to school leaders, superintendents, and board members pushing for these more "rigorous" classrooms. They want "rigorous" lesson design. They want "rigorous" objectives. They say they want to move away from teachers being the "sage on the stage" in favor of them being the "guide on the side" as that's more "rigorous." They push for classes to be more student centered, and they want students to be in collaborative working groups. They want students to pick what projects *they* want to work on, and even the manner in which they'll submit those projects. Again, all because they believe these are more "rigorous" approaches, and that this increase in "rigor" will be the thing that increases student learning.

I did not write this book to argue the merits of direct instruction versus student-centered classrooms. There is a lot of research on both topics, and if you haven't already, I encourage you to seek it out and, of course, make whatever decisions around instruction you need to. However, I also encourage you not to make a premature decision to move to these "more rigorous," student-centered classrooms if your teachers aren't yet expert planners and deliverers of direct instruction. Don't misdiagnose what's happening in your buildings as a need for more rigor, when what your teachers really need is for *you* to coach them on how to intentionally plan, model, and check for understanding in the moment. If, after that, you want your teachers to spend all day in Socratic seminar, go for it. They'll be well-prepared enough to make it happen at a high level.

Teachers move to the next strand when the student outcome goal consistently hits 85 percent or more. The rationale here is that if a teacher has, let's say, 85 percent of students on task, he can still teach, so working on content makes sense, as maybe that last 15 percent are just checked out because the lesson isn't interesting or engaging enough (this is assuming the 15 percent aren't screaming and running around, though they likely wouldn't be as the teacher would be executing on most of the Strand One teacher actions if he has 85 percent on task). If we're at less than 85 percent, working on content won't make much sense. The teacher isn't good enough at the Strand One teacher actions, and he'll struggle with off-task behavior all year if he's pushed forward too quickly. The same goes for Strand Two in a classroom where fewer than 85 percent of students are making progress toward mastering the content. That teacher first needs planning support, and coaching them to push more of the cognitive load onto students at this point would be premature. Even if they're in one strand for weeks or months, the solution cannot be to push someone forward before they're ready. The solution is to coach them more effectively. The teacher actions are not a checklist that need to be worked on one by one, in order. They're more a buffet line, where the leader chooses the skill based solely on the student outcome data collected. If students' transitioning from their desks to the rug takes two minutes, and it's noisy and chaotic (meaning students are off task), teacher action 1.4—*Teacher has created, modeled, and habituated expectations for all class routines (classroom entry, homework submission, share outs, partner work, etc.)*—needs to be worked on. If students aren't making progress toward mastering the content because a clear and precise model wasn't presented to them, then 2.6—*Direct instruction succinctly and efficiently models the precise steps and cognitive process students are expected to take to master content*—is the teacher action to hit. If students aren't deeply engaging with content because all the teacher's questions are basic recall, 3.1—*Teacher scripts out multiple higher-order questions and engagement opportunities in lesson plans. These include opportunities for students to respond to each other*—and 3.3—*After each high-order question asked, teacher will require all students to, either individually or with partners, generate a response (Everybody Writes, Turn and Talk, Whiteboards, etc.)*—should be the focus.

I can't stress this enough as it's the biggest misconception about the framework: Yes, you're training teachers on the specific actions, but the student outcome goal is the sole determinant as to whether you'll push the teacher into the next strand. If you find yourself saying things like, "We just finished 2.8 so it's time for 2.9," you're likely not looking at student outcome data closely enough or using it to drive your decision making.

This framework and approach are designed to help leaders focus on the one (or maybe two) biggest levers for increasing student outcomes, at any one time. The student outcome is what matters and what's measured. The teacher actions are the vehicle to move those student outcomes.

PART TWO:
IGNITION

4
SOUND BITES

You can't do anything if you try to do everything.
—Jen Sincero

If everything is important, then nothing is.
—Patrick Lencioni

The most important thing I learned in all my years of working at Mastery Charter Schools was to focus on student outcomes. To be clear, I write about student outcomes throughout this book, so I'd like to clarify that I'm not talking about outcomes on, for instance, state tests, but rather, outcomes in the classroom itself. I mentioned state tests earlier in reference to my own teaching, more to illustrate a point than anything. But that was the one and only time the conversation about student outcomes, in this book, will pertain to that. There is a ton of debate about the value of state tests (and I have my opinions on the matter), but that's not the conversation I'm having here. Throughout this book, I'll be talking only about what students are doing in the classroom.

It can be easy to default to looking solely at what the teacher is doing when you're in a classroom. This makes sense, as you're *observing* the teacher. But focusing on what the teacher is doing without making the connection to how it's impacting students is only half of the equation. When school leaders do this and then try to give the teacher action steps, it can appear to the teacher that the feedback is random. This can lead to resistance and disinvestment from teachers, as the feedback may seem to be just what the school leader *thinks* or *believes* versus the definitive thing or things that are going to positively impact students.

Here's a nonexample:

Coach: "I'd like you to focus on calling on more students in class."

A teacher hearing this may agree that this is important. Or she may not. Maybe she thinks she already calls on enough students. Either way, this coach hasn't provided nearly enough rationale, in the way of student outcomes, for this action step.

Let's compare that nonexample to this example:

Coach: "You called on six students in class. That means twenty-four students didn't get the opportunity to deeply engage with the content. I'd like us to focus on calling on more students in class, so we can engage more students."

The coach here has made a direct connection between the teacher's actions and the impact on students. Even if the teacher hearing this is exhausted or frustrated or thinking about summer vacation and not at all wanting to add something new to their toolbox, this message is impossible not to hear.

The message, simplified, is this: you can do better for students by doing this thing differently.

This will resonate with every teacher in the world. Whether they'll do it and do it well is another story, but how you can get them there is covered throughout this book. But your first step is to land on the *relationship between teacher actions and student outcomes* in the first place so that you can focus on coaching teachers where they are.

For every teacher and in every observation, you, as a school leader, should be able to land on what we call a "sound bite." This single sentence detailing the relationship between teacher actions and student outcomes is the foundation for all the work you and your teachers will do together.

Here are some examples:

- Students are off task because the teacher does not deliver directions with the attention of the overwhelming majority of students (1.6).

- Students are not mastering the content because an appropriate amount of time hasn't been allocated for each lesson portion to ensure students have enough reps, both guided and independent, to master the content (2.8).

- Students are not deeply engaging with content because the teacher does not require all students to, either individually or with partners, generate a response after all higher-order questions asked (3.3).

These one-sentence sound bites are designed to give you direction and to get teacher buy-in. Often, there will be multiple teacher actions that will lead to an increase in student outcomes. The sound bite is helpful here as it allows you to prioritize. Let's say there's a class where students are significantly off task. The teacher doesn't have a one-voice signal, his directions are too wordy, he doesn't praise, he doesn't scan, and he doesn't redirect students either. In this class, there's *a lot* to work on. This can be overwhelming for both you and the teacher. But even with all the things that need to improve, there is a *first* thing. Because crystal-clear directions delivered to students who aren't paying attention won't land. And scanning a room full of students who haven't heard the directions is a waste of time. Praising kids who likely aren't doing what's been asked (because they didn't hear it) is disingenuous. And while redirection should happen in this class, I'd argue that coaching this teacher on redirection won't set him up for success, as the students *haven't even heard* the directions, and any redirection might be met with major resistance. In this case, the teacher's clear first step is around establishing a one-voice signal.

Here's your sound bite: Students are off task because the teacher does not have a signal (hand raised, countdown, claps, etc.) to achieve and maintain one voice when appropriate (1.5).

To be clear, this teacher still needs to be trained on all the other actions previously mentioned. But he can't get there until this first piece is solidified.

This is a key point. Because I often see this playing out in individual classrooms and schools (and districts) as a whole. There's a paralysis because of how much there is to do. But just like if you and I were charged with fixing up an old house, despite the fact that there'd be dozens of things to work on, there would be a place to start. We might say that the gutters need to be fixed, the back stoop leveled, the walls painted, and so on. All those things might be true and needing of our attention. But focusing on all of them at once wouldn't set us up for success. We'd be spread too thin. We'd be unfocused. So, maybe, in this house, we'd start by ripping up the carpets. Which would allow us to pause on anything else, even if the grass is three feet high and needs to be mowed.

It's important to name here that, if you're going to focus on the causal relationship between what teachers do and what students do as a result, *you* have to believe that relationship exists. Despite the many challenges that educators often face, like overcrowded classrooms, underfunding, poverty, and student trauma, to name a few, *you* have to believe that when adults change *their* actions, students do as well. Maybe it won't be *every* student and it might not happen *right away*, but it happens. I've seen it. I've done it. You may have as well. Working for a turnaround school network for years, I witnessed up close the radical change that can occur for students when adult actions change.

Having a sound bite, whether you present this one sentence directly to teachers or not, will allow you to cut through the noise and focus on the most important current step for increasing student outcomes. This is the first step to coaching teachers *exactly* where they are.

5

COLLECTING DATA

*Without big data, you are blind and deaf
and in the middle of a freeway.*
—Geoffrey Moore

To land on a sound bite, school leaders need to collect data in the classroom. Otherwise, they risk coaching from a place of what they *think* is happening versus what's *definitively* happening. In the next chapter, I'll dive into what, specifically, to collect data on for each strand, but to get started, let me share the first key to collecting data in any classroom: count the students. The moment you walk into a classroom, you should count the students. That number then becomes the denominator in all the data you'll collect. So, for example, this could look like nineteen of twenty-six students are on task, or mastering the content, or deeply engaging with the content. More on this soon.

It is important to collect data on both glows and grows. *Glows* are things that the teacher is executing effectively, and which are therefore contributing to increased student outcomes. *Grows* are things the teacher could do more effectively to further increase student outcomes. Ensure that the data includes student names, time stamps, and direct quotes from students and the teacher. Even if the glows are hard to come by and the grows are too many to count. I once coached a teacher whose initial on-task data was 9 percent. That's right, 9 percent of the students were doing what the teacher asked. As for the other 91 percent, they were yelling, cursing at each other (and the teacher), leaving the room without permission, sitting on the window ledge, standing on chairs, and singing (later that week, one of the students lit up a joint in class and began smoking). The point is, there was very little to celebrate in this class. But I had to find something. And I did. The teacher, despite being frazzled and frustrated (understandably), had a solid routine (1.4) for entering the classroom. So, during entry, on-task was over 50 percent. Still not great, but the fact that his on-task was more than five times higher at this one point, as a result of something *he'd created and executed*, bolstered his pretty low spirits. It also allowed me access, as I was able to say, "Hey, you've increased on-task at that point in the lesson because of something you did. We just need to do that for every point in the lesson." After eight weeks, we got his on-task up to 70 percent. Again, not great and not where I wanted us to get to, but with 70 percent of students on task, he was much better able to teach.

To elaborate more, you may be working with a teacher on differentiating content (2.7). And the teacher may be doing this more effectively (though not perfectly). This teacher may also be highly effective at giving clear directions (1.7) and many other Strand One skills. As such, her on-task percentage is always in the high nineties. It could be tempting to capture *this* as a glow. But if you're in Strand Two, the teacher already knows that the Strand One teacher actions and student outcome are glows. She "graduated" to Strand Two for *this very reason*. So, collecting data around 65 percent of students making progress toward mastering the content—which is up from 48 percent in the previous week because the teacher is now differentiating both in advance and in the moment—will likely resonate more deeply, as it's the very thing you last trained on and it's making a measurable difference.

There's one exception to this rule of ensuring that glows and grows come from the same strand, and that's when a teacher moves from one strand to the next. You likely won't have much Strand Two data if you've just moved from Strand One to Strand Two. This is totally fine. It's great to collect data and then share with a teacher that, as a result of working on teacher actions 1.9 and 1.10, on-task has been consistently over 95 percent, and now it's time to move into Strand Two.

You can also gather powerful data from interviewing students during the lesson. It must be done quickly and delicately, so as not to disrupt students for too long. But questions like the following, asked to students as they're working, can provide great insight into what's happening in the room:

- "What are you working on today?"

- "Why is it important to know how to do this?"

- "What do you have to do to master this?"

- "How close are you to mastering this? How do you know?"

You may find out that students are totally unaware of the day's objective, why it matters, or how to master it. I like to say that in classes like this, school is simply *happening* to the students. They do what's asked because they like and respect the teacher, but they're not truly bought-in and invested in their own learning, because the teacher likely hasn't shared these things in a way that resonates. With this teacher, you would start on 2.4.

If you haven't seen this level of self-awareness from students, I assure you, this is happening in many places. Just recently, I observed first-grade students sharing how they knew they mastered a math lesson. What was even more powerful were the students who shared that they didn't master it, and then provided *evidence* for how they knew they hadn't.

It is important that you make sure your data isn't a false positive. Meaning, if students are taking a test or working on something that's particularly interesting, this could lead to a higher on-task than would typically be seen.

Usually, if students don't listen to the teacher, taking a test doesn't change their behavior *that* much. Still, it's something for you to be aware of, and if you are in the classroom during an atypical lesson or activity, and you sense that what's happening isn't what usually happens, you should return to observe again at a different time.

Often, I get asked about what tool or form should be used to collect data. We intentionally haven't created this because, ultimately, the tool you use is much less important than *what* you collect data on and how you collect it. However, one best practice is *not* to use your computer. This is a shift for some leaders. Using your computer will likely force you to sit down. When you're sitting down, it's harder to provide real-time coaching (which I discuss later on). Also, sitting down and typing likely means you'll be in the room for a longer period of time, which is incongruent with the fast-paced, high-touch approach we prescribe. Also, leaders who type everything out might feel compelled to email their feedback to a teacher. They just did all that work after all. But emailing it means the teacher is now interpreting the feedback without the leader's coaching. The leader won't know if everything is clear. The leader won't know if the teacher agrees. Or if he's totally annoyed. A practice opportunity is also missed. Even if they practice the next time they're together, the teacher has now spent valuable time reviewing a document that isn't guaranteed to move them forward, like a practice session would.

Make sure you're up and active as you're collecting data. Post-it Notes or a small notebook work great as you're circulating the room. Think less about inputting data into a perfect-looking document that you'll email to teachers, and more about collecting precise data on the biggest lever or levers in the room.

6
STRAND-SPECIFIC DATA

It is a capital mistake to theorize before one has data.
—Sherlock Holmes

Collecting data can be daunting if you are unclear as to what you're looking for. However, our framework simplifies this process. Because our framework has three strands, each with one student outcome, and is hierarchical, you only need to look at the student outcomes to find your starting point.

For instance, if you walk into a classroom and half the students aren't doing what the teacher asks, all the data you collect should be around students being on task and the Strand One teacher actions. *On task* can be defined slightly differently from school to school, with some leaders considering raised hands and genuine excitement about the content being representative of students being on task, while some schools may consider it to be simply students following directions. But either way (though I do side more with the latter group), collecting data on content mastery or students' deep engagement with content is pointless at this point. These numbers are *certain* to be low because students aren't on task. We *know* students won't master the content, because they're not listening to the teacher (note: if they are, miraculously, mastering the content despite barely paying attention, the content is way too easy). We know they're not deeply engaging with the content, because they're not even *superficially* engaging with the content.

Here's an example of what the data-collection process in a Strand One classroom could look like. You enter the room and count the students. There are twenty-nine students in the class. You write that down. You notice, immediately, that seven students are talking at the same time the teacher is. You write this down, along with the time it's happening, who the students are (if you know), what they're saying, and what they're supposed to be doing instead. Two students are walking around the room. Again, you write that down, along with what time it's happening, who they are, and what they're supposed to be doing. You begin thinking that this could be a Strand One classroom. The teacher wants students' attention up front and requests it by saying, "Everyone. Everyone. I need you to look up here. Everyone, do this." You jot down this direct quote. You then write down data on how many students give their attention to the teacher. Eleven of twenty-nine are silently (note that the teacher didn't ask them to be silent so this will be a data point as well) looking up at the board. You collect data on what the other students are doing. James and Tanya are throwing papers at each other. Eli tells Angel to "Shut up!" right in front of the teacher. No redirection occurs. This is clearly a Strand One classroom. You continue to collect on-task data every five minutes and after every all-group task. You collect direct quotes from students and the teacher, including three examples of the teacher praising students who are working. This is important as, despite this teacher's struggles, you'll want to have positive data as well. You collect data on student actions. You use time stamps for everything.

Here's an additional example of data you could collect in a Strand One room:

At 8:14, the teacher says, "Please silently copy today's objective. Take 20 seconds." Teacher is not looking at students when directions are given (looking through papers on cart).

Within 30 seconds of the direction being given, eight of twenty-nine students have begun.

Tajae and Willie began immediately.

The teacher does not see this (looking through papers).

Seth is playing drums on his desk.

Maria is walking around the room.

Daisy calls out, "I hate this class."

The teacher does not redirect the off-task students, as she's not looking at them (now looking at her laptop).

A total of twelve of twenty-nine students copy the objective. It takes longer than two minutes.

Sound Bite: Students are off task because the teacher doesn't scan the room after every direction to determine whether or not behavioral expectations are being met. Teacher action 1.8.

If you've determined, however, that the classroom is not Strand One, the next step is to determine if the students understand the material being presented, and if they're making progress toward mastering it. This data can be gathered by sampling student work, during guided and independent practice. You would do this by circulating the room and reviewing, somewhat briefly, a large enough sample size that the data likely wouldn't be random, but a small enough sample size that it would be manageable to collect. Five to ten students is what I suggest for a classroom of between twenty and thirty students. While circulating, make note of how many students, out of the total number sampled, are making progress. This is a little trickier than gauging on-task which is relatively easy to observe. And as I shared earlier, all students mastering the content isn't necessarily a good thing, as the lesson might be too easy. If that were the case, you'd still collect data and share some version of the following, during the meeting: "Ten of ten students sampled had the objective mastered. However, you didn't model a skill, and the independent practice was a matching exercise that students were able to complete without direct instruction. That tells me the objective should have challenged them more." This would still be a Strand Two classroom as the lesson objective is not the most important next step for students (2.1).

Remember, teachers have to have *taught* a process (even just a targeted reteach of a previously taught skill) for content mastery to be gauged. If they haven't, progress toward mastery is almost impossible to assess because there's no *criteria* for mastery. It's like driving without a destination. But this is okay, because a teacher in this situation would be started in Strand Two and you would begin working with them on 2.1, 2.2, and eventually 2.6.

Below is a chart with some sample Strand Two glow and grow data:

GLOW	GROW
Objective: Students will be able to determine the root causes of WW2 Previous Student Outcome Goal: When asked, 60% of students sampled will be able to name the objective and what they have to do to master it. Previous Teacher Goal: Teacher will reference the objective and what students will need to do to master it, a minimum of four times per lesson. Teacher Actions: 2.4 and 2.10 Sampled from 11:10–11:19. 7/8 (87.5%) knew the objective. Lanae said it verbatim. Sammy was one word off. 6/8 (75%) knew the criteria: annotate for three causes, two European, one US, game changers. Lanae, Sammy, Amir, Julio, Lisa, and Cece. One reference of objective at 10:55. You ask a student to read it, all students copy it. Then make a prediction about what the causes could be (100% on task). Three more references: 11:00, 11:05, 11:17 Goal Hit	3/8 mastered/were mastering (Germany invades Czechoslovakia, Germany invades Poland, Japan bombs Pearl Harbor). Sampled from 11:22 – 11:31. 2/8 knew two causes (Sammy/Cece—missing Pearl Harbor). 1/8 knew one cause (Kimberly—had Pearl Harbor) 11:10: Asked kids to work in pairs to annotate. "With a partner, annotate for as many game-changing causes as you can find." (on-task was 68%, two minutes into this). **No model occurs in the lesson.** Grow Teacher Action: 2.6 (Direct instruction succinctly and efficiently models the precise steps and cognitive process students are expected to take to master content.)

Strand Three data collection should be focused around the depth of teacher questioning, how often those questions are asked, and how deeply all students engage with them. You will want to collect data on the total number of questions asked and what percentage of those rise beyond the level of basic recall, naming, or listing. The questions asked should challenge students to comprehend, apply, analyze, synthesize, or evaluate the material presented. You will want to collect data on how often the teacher is talking versus how often the students are writing and responding to each other. How often the teacher responds to students versus how often students respond to each other is great data to collect as well.

See below for an example of glow-and-grow Strand Three data:

GLOW	GROW
Previous Student Outcome Goal: 85% of students making progress toward mastering the content as assessed in both GP and IP.	Twenty-two questions over three observations—all but one were recall, calculation, listing, labeling (not including the extension exercises).
Teacher Actions: 2.7 and 2.9	Teacher responded to all students first.
Extension Work Example: Compare and contrast the effects of gravity on the moon vs. multiple other planets. For students who are moving quickly/modifications for students who require them, ask for two ways gravity is different on the moon.	Average amount of time students were working on higher-level material (not copying the objective, etc.) was 24% of each lesson.
Collecting data in both GP and IP in all three lessons. Minimum seven students (pushing kids back to the steps). Used new approach in second lesson.	Grow Teacher Action: 3.1 (Teacher scripts out multiple higher-order questions and engagement opportunities in lesson plans. These include opportunities for students to respond to each other.)
Three observations, avg. of 91% mastering content: 93%, 93%, 90%.	

PART THREE:
LAUNCH

7
PREPARATION

*One important key to success is self-confidence.
An important key to self-confidence is preparation.*
—Arthur Ashe

You've now collected a lot of great data, and you've landed on your teacher's sound bite. The next step is to meet with the teacher to share your findings and to practice the skill that will most improve student outcomes. As I referenced earlier, this might be a shift for some school leaders who'd prefer, either to save time or because it's exponentially easier, to simply send an email or drop a note with data and some suggested next steps in the teacher's mailbox. Alert! Alert! This is *not* coaching! Imagine if a dance coach didn't give his dancer's feedback in person, but instead, he sent each of them emails after practice with some things they could or should do differently. Would the dancers change their habits? Would the coach be certain they knew *how* to change their habits? Would the coach be confident in holding them accountable for making the changes he shared? The answer to each of these questions is almost certainly "no." And it's the same with school leaders and teachers.

Here are the questions from earlier that coaches should be asking themselves after every coaching meeting. Again, we coach our school leaders to be able to answer in the affirmative to each of the questions below after every meeting:

- Did that teacher just get significantly better at something?

- Do they know their next steps?

- Have I put systems in place so I'm able to hold them accountable?

Remember, if the answer to any of these questions is a *no*, we know the meeting could have been more impactful. Coaching is about intentionally and strategically building skill. It's not about leaving notes and hoping. But to be able to answer "yes" to the questions above, to avoid the hoping, we need to be incredibly well prepared on the front end.

There are four components that you should have prepped in advance of a coaching meeting to ensure it's as effective as possible: meeting agenda, weekly goals, practice activity, and next steps.

MEETING AGENDA

I can tell one minute into any meeting if the meeting is going to be effective. The tell isn't about how well the people in the meeting relate to each other or how excited they seem. The tell is in the delivery on the front end, by the person running lead, of the agenda and the intended outcomes of their time together.

Too few coaching meetings begin with the school leader saying something that sounds like, "So here's what we're going to do today." But they should.

We'll get into the *delivery* of the full agenda in chapter ten, but for now, the goal for you is to come prepared with an agenda that includes both glow and grow data and a practice activity with criteria, goals, and next steps, so you can maximize every second you're with your teachers.

Please see the example below:

SAMPLE MEETING AGENDA (COACH VERSION)

- CHECK-IN

- GLOW: 100 percent of students, across multiple observations, could name the day's objective and what they had to do to master it. Area to celebrate: 2.4. (Sienna: three main ideas and a clear intro paragraph. Jasmine: a clear introduction with three main ideas.)

- PREVIOUS WEEKLY STUDENT OUTCOME GOAL: 65 percent of students will show progress toward mastery of the objective (baseline from five weeks ago was 27 percent). Teacher Action: 2.6 (Direct instruction succinctly and efficiently models the precise steps and cognitive process students are expected to take to master content.)
Data based on multiple observations this week: 70 percent of students showed progress. 80 percent in period 1, 65 percent in period 2, and 65 percent in period 3. *Goal met but proficiency in Strand Two not achieved.*

- GROW: Significant practice time (2.8). Period 1 had four minutes to practice, period 2 had two minutes, period 3 had two minutes. On average, 30 percent of students had completed less than half of the independent work at the time the period ended. The sample size was small, and teacher did not have time to circulate and check for understanding to adjust instruction, because pacing was off. This is all due to the do now in each class (across multiple days) taking an average of more than twenty-two minutes to complete and review.

- SOUND BITE: Students aren't making significant progress toward mastering the objective because they don't have enough time for GP and IP (2.8).

- ACTION STEP: The entire do now needs to be completed and reviewed in under ten minutes.

- PRACTICE: Coach modified previous day's do now to remove less important questions. Also, two questions were chosen to review as opposed to ten. Rationale given is that they're the most important questions for gauging student understanding. Teacher will modify next three days' do nows by both removing less important question and choosing which questions to review. Coach will provide feedback.

- NEW WEEKLY STUDENT OUTCOME GOAL/S: On average, more than 85 percent of students will complete the independent practice by the end of the period.

- 80 percent of students will show significant progress toward mastering the objective.

- TEACHER GOAL: Do now takes under ten minutes to complete (including review).

- NEXT STEPS:

- Teacher will script all do nows in lesson plans the same way going forward and will submit to coach by end of day each Friday.

- Coach will observe teacher Monday, period 1; Tuesday, periods 3 and 7; and Wednesday, period 2.

- Coach will have timer running at the beginning of each do now and give a signal as each minute passes.

- Coach will give real-time feedback advising teacher to move on if she's spending too much time on one question.

- Coach and teacher will meet Wednesday, period 8 to share data and plan next steps.

Having an agenda that's this well planned out will allow for a smoother and more deliberate meeting. To be clear, the physical agenda copy doesn't need to be shared with the teacher, so you don't need to spend hours creating it to make sure it's perfectly formatted and pleasing to the eye. In fact, you can write it in pencil on a piece of loose-leaf if that works for you. And it shouldn't take you more than thirty minutes to create, either (this is initially; you'll get faster), as you'll already have all the data. What matters is that, just like a person driving cross-country, you have a road map for your meeting. You may diverge slightly at points, but ultimately, this agenda will keep you on track until you reach your destination.

WEEKLY GOALS

If I asked you to go for a run, the very first question you'd ask me would be "How far?" If I asked you to go for a drive you'd ask, "To where?" It's human nature. We want to know what's for dinner, or what movie we're going out to watch, or what time the event starts. The same goes for setting goals for students and teachers in coaching meetings. Teachers should know the goals, so they know where they're headed. And the more precise these goals are, the more easily you can collect data on them and celebrate progress along the way.

Using the data you collected and the sound bite you landed on, you'll set a goal for the teacher and her students. These goals are what we call *now goals*. These now goals are the goals you'll try to hit over the week to follow, or maybe two. The larger *later goals* will drive your work for the entire coaching cycle. Let's say that in your initial observation of a teacher, the data says that 25 percent of students are making progress toward mastering the content. You decide that your later goal will be to have 70 percent of the students consistently making progress toward mastering the content. Which means that's the goal you'll hit by the end of your time together. That's rigorous but likely attainable. To get there, though, you'd set a now goal for each week around what the teacher will do, and then set a corresponding student outcome goal that you'll try to hit as a result.

For now, let's focus on *now* student outcome goals and their corresponding teacher goals:

SAMPLE STUDENT OUTCOME GOALS	SAMPLE TEACHER GOALS
1. 60% of students will be on task	1. Teacher gives directions that include time, task, materials, and sound for 4 out of every 5 directions given
2. 3/5 students can name the objective and why it's important	2. Teacher references the objective and why it matters 3X before DI
3. 75% of students will deeply engage with content, 5X or more	3. Teacher will give a written task after 80% of higher-order questions.
4. 80% of students will be on task within fifteen seconds of directions being given	4. Teacher will give TTMS (time, task, materials, and sound) directions, scan, and praise for three students within 10 seconds of directions being given
5. 70% of students will be on task within ten seconds of do now directions being given	5. Teacher will give TTMS directions, scan, and praise for three students within 10 seconds of the do now beginning

These rigorous but attainable goals should be included in your agenda (as you likely just noticed when you reviewed our sample one). Make sure you design them in advance, based on the current data you have.

PRACTICE ACTIVITY

This is such a big topic, it could probably be its own chapter. I have it here because of how important it is to ensure your practice session is planned out in advance. Big picture: You must practice with your teachers if you want them to move rapidly. And to practice, you must be prepared with a model and criteria for what makes your model effective.

Most school leaders do not ask their teachers to practice. This is largely because they think practice will be uncomfortable, or because they're not confident in their ability to model effectively and provide precise feedback. Some leaders think it's disrespectful. Teachers are professionals after all. If that's your mindset, I encourage you to shift your focus away from *your* feelings and *your teachers'* feelings and toward your schoolwide goals, what's best for students, and the commitment you made to their families. Practice is like a lot of things in schools: it lives or dies in the framing of it. You can normalize practice and the idea that you and your entire team are committed to continuously improving yourselves for your students. You can have teachers watch you receive coaching from a colleague. You can say that Michael Jordan practiced all the time. Misty Copeland practices now all the time. Doctors practice their incisions on cadavers. Lawyers practice their opening and closing statements in front of colleagues. A lot of professionals practice. It's how they get better.

When designing your practice, first ensure that your practice session is aligned to the sound bite and corresponding teacher action you're working on. If the teacher needs to work on scanning, the practice should be on scanning. If she needs to work on differentiation, the practice should be on differentiation.

Next, decide if it'll be what we call a "get-up-and-say-it" session or a scripting session. For some teacher actions, this is simple. Teacher action 2.1 (*Lesson objective is the most important next step for students; all materials selected are purposeful, rigorous, and aligned to that objective.*) is *only* about scripting, so your decision there would be easy. However, if you look at 1.4 (*Teacher has created, modeled, and habituated expectations for all class routines.*), for instance, you'll need to know if the teacher has created routines but not modeled or explained them to students, versus the teacher not having ever created them in the first place. If it's the former, you'd choose a get-up-and-say-it session. If it's the latter, you'd practice by scripting.

After that, create a model to make sure you can present to teachers what this looks like when done well. And make sure you design clear criteria for what makes yours an effective model. We use a simple but memorable term for this: *what makes the thing the thing?* To be able to point out to the teacher precisely what you're doing in your model, you'll need to plan this in advance. Otherwise, your session will be less effective than it can be. This is important as there are degrees of effectiveness of practice in coaching meetings, and what I'm describing is the *most* effective.

- Ineffective: "You should give clearer directions." (no model, no practice)

- Minimally Effective: "You should give clearer directions. Let's practice it now." (no model from coach, teacher practices, no feedback given)

- Moderately Effective: "You should give clearer directions. Let me model [*coach models*]. What did you notice? Now it's your turn." (coach models, no criteria shared, teacher provides some criteria, teacher practices, no feedback given)

- Highly Effective: "Let's practice giving clear directions. I'm going to model. Look for these five things: I'm going to name the time the students have, what the specific task is, what the sound level is, and what materials they'll need to be successful. Also, I'm going to make eye contact with students in the room to ensure I have their attention. Watch me [*coach models*]. Now it's your turn. I'll provide feedback as you're going." (coach models, criteria shared, teacher practices, specific feedback about criteria given)

Finally, make sure to pull back on scaffolds as you're designing to make the practice increasingly harder, and to allow for more reps for the teacher. You'll likely need to take more time on the first example as the teacher perfects her language (either written or verbal), which is fine. But by the end of the session, you should be in rapid-fire mode. If we use the example of clear directions, perhaps the session starts with the above model and then progresses to the teacher practicing this example five or ten times. Then, you provide a new scenario and the teacher practices again for five to ten reps. But soon, you give a scenario and the teacher is, on the fly, coming up with and delivering clear directions. And again, with a new scenario. Then again. The goal is to build automaticity. To build a habit. And designing this increasingly more intense approach will support that.

There's one additional note on practice design I'd like to share here. If you're coaching a teacher in Strand One, it's very likely you'll be designing a get-up-and-say-it practice at some point. And in those practices, teachers are sometimes asked to redirect students (teacher action 1.10). While it may be tempting (and easy) to choose real student names as you're designing, you should avoid this. A high-rep practice could have a teacher "redirecting" using the same student's name dozens of times. This could potentially lead a teacher to believe that this student is a troublemaker (or reinforce that belief). After all, you chose this student to be part of the practice. This is of course, problematic as you're trying to illustrate for the teacher that he's the lever, and that when he does X differently, students will do Y differently. If you use a student's name, you could undermine yourself (not to mention, do a major disservice to the student whose name you used). Use your own name or even the name of an actress or actor instead.

PREPARATION

NEXT STEPS

After every meeting, you'll have next steps for both yourself and the teacher. Make sure you plan these in advance. When is the next meeting? Observation? Will the teacher be scripting more directions? Objectives? Higher-order questions? Will they go see the teacher down the hall who's an expert at designing and delivering lesson hooks and then send you a reflection?

To be clear, this is not busywork and you won't impose deadlines for the sake of deadlines. You want to make sure that every teacher you're coaching is in a constant state of practicing and learning. The goal is to design the next steps so that their growth isn't isolated to *only* the time they're with you.

Think about someone who sees a personal trainer. Maybe they meet with that trainer once or twice per week. But the trainer also gives them a diet plan to follow. She also asks that they read an article about fasting while jotting down anything that resonates with them. Maybe they keep a food and workout diary, all to be shared at the beginning of the next session. This level of support, if followed, will increase this person's gains. But the personal trainer is at a disadvantage, as they likely can't set hard-and-fast deadlines for their client. *They* work for the client. The trainer would have trouble holding their client accountable if they didn't follow through on one of the action steps. But your teachers work *for you*, and you can set those deadlines and hold them accountable for meeting them.

8
COMMUNICATION

When bosses are too invested in everyone getting along, they also fail to encourage the people on their team to criticize one another for fear of sowing discord. They create the kind of work environment where being "nice" is prioritized at the expense of critiquing, and therefore improving, actual performance.
—Kim Malone Scott

You can have brilliant ideas, but if you can't get them across, your ideas won't get you anywhere.
—Lee Iacocca

One of the things that makes our model different than nearly every other coaching model out there is our approach to communication and providing feedback. When it comes to communicating with and providing feedback to teachers, most coaching models prescribe the use of probing questions to lead teachers to a deeper understanding of their own growth areas.

It sounds like this:
- "You had five of twenty-one students following your directions. Why do you think that was?"

- "Eleven of twenty-four students understood the steps you modeled. What do you think the other students missed?"

- "How did you come up with those questions? What could make them more engaging?"

And so on.

Why do school leaders engage in these kinds of meetings? The first thing leaders share with me is that they want to empower their teachers. That it's better for the teachers if they figure it out on their own, with some support from us. We could argue whether this is true or not. But let's say there is value for teachers in this approach. Who loses here? It's students, of course. If you have one coaching meeting per week with a teacher, half of which is spent trying to get the teacher to an understanding that you can simply *share with them* on the front end, and then practice time is minimal or nonexistent as a result, kids lose. Yes, the teacher may have a greater theoretical understanding of the skill (or not), but they likely won't be any *better* at it. Schools of education are overflowing with theory, while often being thin on execution. Well, this is the perfect time to practice executing.

Next, leaders share that they don't want to offend or upset their teachers by telling them what to do. I could argue that these leaders are actually more worried about how *they'll* feel if their employees are angry or annoyed by them. And I'm certain I'd be right at least some of the time. But that's irrelevant. What is relevant, however, is that the problem of not wanting to offend teachers is solved through the use of a digestible framework that makes classroom analysis simple, with strong communication, observable student results to keep motivation high, and the framing of coaching on the front end (chapter eleven).

These reasons for not simply sharing what a teacher needs to do to be more effective come up a lot. In the worst-case scenarios, they're used by school leaders who lack the confidence and instructional expertise to name the thing, why it matters, and what it looks like when done well; by leaders who lack the confidence to ask their teachers to practice something; and by leaders who arrive underprepared to meetings with the hope that the teachers will give them enough help, through their responses, for the leader to be able to fake it through until the end.

In the best-case scenarios, they're used by leaders who truly believe this approach makes sense. Often, these leaders have been trained on Adult Learning Theory (or they're at least familiar with it). I won't dive into it too deeply here, but the gist is that adults learn differently than children. Adult Learning Theory states that adults need to see the relevance in what they're learning. That they learn best when they're part of the solution. They have life experiences that they can draw from that can aid their development and help with problem-solving.

Let me be clear. I started Skyrocket, in part, to serve as an alternative to this approach. I've observed hundreds of these meetings and a few trends emerge from them. First, these meetings meander far more often than more directive meetings do, as the coaches often have to engage in conversations that are not aligned to their predetermined focus areas. Next, these meetings do not drive hard enough at tangible outcomes. This makes sense, as the teacher and the coach gradually land on the best next step together. Which makes coming prepared with criteria, practice, and goals much more difficult. And finally, these meetings often do not lead to *radical improvement* in teachers, as practice time is either minimized or, in many of these probing meetings, nonexistent.

If we assume the best of our teachers, we must assume that if they knew how to do the thing they need to do to impact students more, they'd do it. So, we should spend the finite amount of time we have with them simply telling them what to do and then practicing it. Because in reality, they're not really "learning" these things from you, which makes Adult Learning Theory largely irrelevant here. What you're *actually* doing is training them on the schoolwide expectations for positive classroom culture, effective instruction, and student engagement. So, this is less like someone learning a foreign language and more like a pilot being trained on exactly how to take off, to lift the landing gear, and to climb. The instructor in this case simply tells her student what direction to head, what speed will be optimal, and what levers should be pulled. These things aren't fluid. They're static, because they're the most effective way to do these things. While there's room in here for the pilot to do some things his own way and to have some ownership, there are some pieces that are just so.

As an example, there are dozens of techniques a teacher can use to get students' attention. But what's undeniable, what no person in education could ever argue, is that teachers do need to be able to get students' attention to be effective. If the pilot wants to blast Metallica as he's taking off (once he's good enough), that's fine. What's not up for debate is the speed he needs to hit to get the plane airborne. This holds true for nearly everything in schools, and you should feel confident sharing these things in this very direct way.

As for relevance and motivation, wanting to do what's best for the hundreds of students in your schools should be providing that.

That's why our approach is directive. We tell teachers, using precise data, what they need to do to be more effective for students. Then we coach them to do it. And sure, there's room in a coaching meeting to say something like, "Okay, here's my script for directions. This is the language I use, but I want you to feel really comfortable, so please script out how *you* would say it." And if a teacher is in Strand Three, likely the coaching would be more collaborative, as that person is more advanced. But we don't need to probe as to why a teacher hasn't created an entry routine or why a teacher isn't checking for understanding throughout every lesson. They just need to be told to do it, shown how to it, and then coached on how to master it. *This* approach will ultimately empower teachers, as they'll get better more quickly, gaining confidence as they do. And *this* approach will ultimately empower students, as they'll have more access to the material, increasing their skill and knowledge along the way.

To hammer home this point, imagine if you brought your car in to get worked on and instead of being able to pick it up the next day, you were told it would take four days because the boss wants the new mechanic to "figure out" what's wrong with it. She's studied Adult Learning Theory and she wants the mechanic to pull on his life experiences to find a solution for what's wrong with your car. You'd be livid or shocked and would likely take your business elsewhere. Well, students and families (our "customers") often don't even know this is happening. But *we* know. And, we can't be okay with students losing a week or a month or a year of excellent schooling because we want to "empower" their teachers.

So, let's tell teachers what to do in a way that truly empowers and inspires them. Let's do that using our DASH Communication Framework, which is data-focused, authentic, straight, and helpful:

Data-focused: Data must be the root of all communication. Remove any judgmental words and focus only on what's happening in the class.

Authentic: Share yourself with the person. Your likes, your dislikes, your grow areas. They should get to know *you* in the process.

Straight: There's nothing to hide. Don't sugarcoat anything. Don't qualify. Don't make excuses for the teacher or the students.

Helpful: We are going to do this together. I will support you in getting there.

Look at these three examples presenting the same data to a teacher:

Example 1:
"It seems like the kids were having an off day today. What do you think? I counted six students on task, but it was kind of hard to tell from where I was. I'm sure it's usually higher. I know you're really working hard with them. And it was first period. But still, why do you think they struggled today? What do you think you could have done differently?"

Example 2:
"Today was tough. Only six out of twenty-nine students were listening to you. You're not in charge in the class. You barely had students' attention when you gave directions, and you need to fix that because the students deserve better. I need you to focus on getting students to pay attention to you to ensure all students do what you ask."

Example 3:
"Six out of twenty-nine students were consistently on task in the lesson. I know that you know that we need to get that up. If we work together to ensure you have students' attention before you

deliver directions, I'm confident we can get more of them on task. This might not be easy, but we're going to do it together to ensure all students are successful. I struggled with this when I was a teacher. And I got great at it. We *will* increase your effectiveness on this."

The differences between the first and second examples and the third are both subtle and obvious, but the third is much more effective. On the more subtle side, the third coach removes words like "only" and "barely," as those words are judgmental and unnecessary. If sharing with a teacher that six out of twenty-nine students were on task doesn't jolt them, if it doesn't paint a clear picture that what's happening is not okay, then perhaps there's a different conversation about schoolwide expectations that needs to occur. The third coach removes these judgments and simply shares the data about precisely what's happening in the room.

On the more obvious side, the third coach uses words like, "we" and "together" to illustrate that she's going to support the teacher in being successful. She's being helpful here. She also replaces the word "fix" with the term "increase your effectiveness," as fix implies that something is broken. But the teacher *is able* to get six students to stay on task. Which means he's likely doing something or some things effectively. Or maybe he's just not doing everything ineffectively. Either way, "increase your effectiveness" means we're building on the thing that's currently there. Again, removing judgmental words and sticking to data.

The coach in the third conversation, while clearly more supportive, doesn't sugarcoat things the way the first coach does. She doesn't qualify her feedback by saying, "I know you're really working hard with them" or "the kids are having an off day." Those things may be true, but it doesn't *actually* matter. What does matter is that the teacher is not providing students with what they need to be successful and that his coach is going to support him in getting there. So, she states the data simply and clearly and then discusses how they're going to get better together.

Finally, the coach shares how she also struggled with this once. Not every conversation will lend itself to this, but some will, and coaches should feel comfortable sharing authentically here.

One potential shift to a conversation like this would occur if the teacher were simply refusing to execute on action steps. If he, despite being expertly trained for at least a few weeks, wasn't doing what he was trained on. Then the coach would be justified in changing tone. But for the overwhelming majority of meetings, a supportive conversation grounded in data will be most positively received.

Here's a quick language cheat sheet that includes judgmental words or phrases to avoid on the left and less judgmental words on the right that you can swap in as replacements:

It was bad	Less effective than it could be
Need to make it better	We can make it more effective/impactful
The transition was too slow	It was less urgent than it could be
We need the do now review to be faster	We can make it more urgent
The lesson was too easy	We need to make it more rigorous

I'd like to close the chapter by flagging four communication pitfalls that every coach should avoid: I like/I love language, apology language, low-bar language, and imprecise language.

COMMUNICATION

I LIKE/I LOVE LANGUAGE

Do your best to avoid language that includes terms like "I like" or "I love." It's great if you like what's happening in the classroom; however, ask yourself *why* you like or love it? Is it because students are doing X or Y differently because of it? If so, share that.

Look at these two examples:
Example 1:
"I love the way you're questioning students now."

Example 2:
"You're asking all students to write a response after every higher-order question you ask. As a result, 100 percent of students deeply engaged with content four times in the lesson."

The first example might leave teachers striving to please *you*. They may think that the things they do just need to meet your bar and stop there. However, the second example makes a direct connection between the teacher's actions and their impact on student outcomes.

You can even add the "love" piece if the second example is too dry for you:

You're asking all students to write a response after every higher-order question you ask. As a result, 100 percent of students deeply engaged with content four times in the lesson. I love that because kids are really benefitting from it.

Just remember to include how the thing you "love" is connected to an increase in student performance.

APOLOGY LANGUAGE

Imagine you buy tickets to a play you've been wanting to see for months. On the night of the show, right as the performance is about to start, one of the actors steps out and says, "Thanks so much for being here. I know it's late and you're probably tired. And I know you're very busy and have a lot of stuff to do at home. For both those reasons, we'll make the show quick so you can get home early. Thanks again."

You'd be totally disinvested, wondering why you should sit through the play at all. Well, this happens *all the time* in coaching meetings. We tell teachers, "I don't want to take too much of your time," and "I don't want to make extra work for you," and "This will be quick because I know you have a lot of stuff to do." And *then* we expect them to be *excited* to meet with us!

We say these things because we want to acknowledge the very real pressures and time constraints that teachers are facing. But in doing so, we totally undermine ourselves by positioning what we're doing not as an awesome experience that will make the teacher more effective, but as an extra thing that they need to endure so that they can get back to their real work.

You can acknowledge that someone is busy without undermining yourself by doing the following:

1. Reference students.
2. Assume the best.
3. Thank them in advance.

Watch how the apologies from earlier are rewritten. Teachers will feel that you get how busy they are while also understanding the importance of the work you're about to engage in.

"I don't want to take too much of your time" becomes "Thanks for the time. You're always up for anything when it comes to supporting kids."

"I don't want to make extra work for you" becomes "Thanks in advance for doing the extra work. It's going to make a difference for you and your students."

"This will be quick because I know you have a lot of stuff to do" becomes "This is really important for you and your students, so thanks for your attention as we're working together."

In addition to not wanting to "burden" teachers with more stuff to do, leaders sometimes apologize because they're unsure of their own ability. Sometimes it's because they're intimidated by the teacher and worried about their response. Maybe they had a bad experience in the past with this teacher. Sometimes it's because they're unprepared, so they're already predicting a bad meeting. Or it could be because of poor framing up front, or because they used to teach together and now there's a weird power dynamic.

Ultimately, it doesn't matter. It's not helpful. You're an expert coach who's charged with making your teachers more effective for students. And as one of my principals shared recently with a teacher who was overwhelmed by some of her coaching requests: "This isn't happening to you. It's *for you.*"

LOW-BAR LANGUAGE

The most toxic kind of language in schools is what I call *low-bar language*. It's a thing that adults in school buildings say to place blame for poor performance (theirs or the students') on *others* and *other things* versus taking responsibility for it.

These seemingly innocuous excuses are often used as reasons for why things aren't going well. Have you ever heard one of these? Have you ever used one?

"It's first period."
"It's last period."

"It's almost summer break."
"It's right after summer break."
"It's raining out."
"It's beautiful out."
"It's right before lunch."
"It's right after lunch."
"We're about to have an assembly."
"We just had an assembly."
"It's almost state testing."
"We just had state testing."
"It's almost Thanksgiving (or insert holiday here)."
"It's right after Thanksgiving (or insert holiday here)."
"We just had a snow day."
"We might have a snow day."
"We just had a long weekend."
"It was a short week."
"It's Friday."
"It's early."
"It's late."
"It's Daylight Savings."

If we listen closely, there are dozens and dozens of "things" we can use as excuses for our districts, networks, schools, and individual classrooms being average (or worse).

But all these excuses, even if some are grounded in reality, do nothing to empower the adults in our buildings to embrace always being great for students. They do nothing to encourage adults to *own* the idea that despite what's currently happening, *our* actions can still make a difference.

How about these statements *about kids* from adults to other adults?

"That's my tough class."
"She's special ed."
"That won't work for my students."
"James never does anything. Even in Ms. Jones's class."
"Those are the low kids."

Referring to students as high or low in general is something I suggest you avoid and coach teachers to avoid. I work with a school team in Philadelphia who refers to students, when needed, as either highly prepared, prepared, or underprepared on a *specific* topic (multiplying fractions for instance versus math in general). This way, they've put the onus on the adults to get them to a place of being highly prepared and don't risk dismissing an entire class or even one student because they may be struggling with one particular skill.

What about this statement?

They're a good class.

Wait, you might be thinking, "What could possibly be wrong with this one? It's a compliment!" It could be. It could also imply that other classes *aren't* good. And it also implies that students are just who they are and that *our actions* don't factor into that. If they're a "good class" just because they're a good class, what's my motivation to work harder or differently with the "tough class"? Because that's just who *they* are too. If the reason why the "high class" is doing great on the assignment is *because* they're the "high class," and we all *agree* that that's why, then, when the "low class" doesn't do as well and we attribute it to them being the "low class," we place the blame on the students and let ourselves off the hook.

One use of low-bar language isn't toxic, but hundreds sure can be. They can lead to a culture where adults think student success is left to chance. Which doesn't mean some things in schools aren't true (or relatively true). If you argue that it *is* harder to teach a class right after lunch than it is to teach right before lunch, I'd likely agree. If you tell me that it gets harder to engage students as the weather changes from cold to warm, again, I'd likely agree. But then I'd ask, "Is it impossible?" Because if it's not impossible, it just means we need to do better. We need to be more effective during those classes and times of year. Just like if someone tasked the two of us with building a rocket ship to the moon, we might struggle and ultimately fail. But we wouldn't *ever* be able to say it's impossible. We *know* it's not impossible, because it's been done. So, if we can't do it, we just need to learn how. Because even though Mr. Smith is struggling with the seventh graders, maybe Ms. Clark has great classes with them. Which means it is possible. And if it's possible, but we're not able to do it right now, it just means we're not there yet. But it also means it's *on us* to get there.

IMPRECISE LANGUAGE

Years ago, I was sitting with three principals from the same charter school network in Atlanta. One was the elementary principal, one was the middle school principal, and the third, the high school principal. They were debating a schoolwide (meaning K–12) initiative, and they all had a slightly different idea about how this new thing should be messaged. They asked me my opinion. They wanted to see who I sided with.

I responded, "It doesn't matter. You just need choose and then be 100 percent aligned with your messaging and language around it."

Our Strand One student outcome is on-task. But some schools refer to on-task as engagement, while others refer to it as students being bought-in, or on board, or attentive. All of these are fine, just like all the ideas those Atlanta principals had were fine. Just choose your language and then norm it so everyone uses it.

The more you can minimize and even eliminate confusing and inconsistent language, the less time the people on your team will need to spend on figuring out what others are saying.

Whether you use our framework or a different one, have it *at* your coaching meetings. Make sure the teachers have copies. Refer to it often. Read the teacher actions out loud. Have the teachers do the same. And whether you call it an objective, or a learning target, or an essential question, make sure you land on normed language and then use *only* that.

Finally, and this is specifically for leaders who *are using* or *plan to use* our framework, make sure your language across the strands is consistent. Meaning, if you're talking about directions (1.7), all the data shared needs to be aligned to students being on task (or not). If you want a teacher to check for understanding more effectively (2.9), it has to be driving at more students mastering the content. And if you want teachers to model and hold students accountable for using academic language (3.7), make sure it's in service of driving up opportunities for all students to deeply engage with the content.

Many leaders feel most comfortable talking about on-task as it's the easiest to observe. So, what can happen is that everything the leader shares relates back to students doing or not doing what was asked. "You modeled the skill and twenty-four of twenty-four kids were on task." This is great data, however, it's imprecise as it's a Strand Two teacher action and the Strand One student outcome.

This kind of coaching can lead to confusion and words not meaning nearly as much as they should. Too much of that and people become numb to your messages. If on-task also means engagement *and* bought-in, and Strand One and Strand Two teacher actions lead to the *same* student outcome *sometimes but not always*, the specificity and precision of this model (or others) are lost.

9
ACCOUNTABILITY

Accountability separates the wishers in life from the action-takers that care enough about their future to account for their daily actions.
—John Di Lemme

I'd like to begin this chapter by sharing the story of a fictional coach named Ray. A teacher shows up late to Ray's meeting. It's only two minutes, which isn't really a big deal. But Ray never shared that it's important to get to meetings on time. He never shared this as an expectation. And the teacher is really stressed. So, Ray doesn't say anything. The next time the teacher shows up five minutes late. Stressed again. But now Ray feels foolish saying something because he didn't say something the first time the teacher showed up late. Ray feels totally disempowered and defaults to asking questions about the teacher's stress level. "Are you okay?" "Is there anything you need?"

The teacher says, "No. But I just have so much to do. Is this going to be fast?"

Ray begins to dread meeting with this teacher, who vacillates between showing up five to ten minutes late and not showing up at all. And when the teacher does show up, this person is always angry and unprepared. The teacher stomps into the room empty-handed. No computer. No notebook. No pen. No coaching framework. So, Ray spends their precious time together acting as a friend and confidant. Because it's the only thing that makes him feel useful. The teacher unloads to Ray about everything that's wrong with the school. And Ray doesn't say anything. He's completely powerless. The teacher is in total control of the meetings. Of the relationship. Ray feels ridiculous at this point asking the teacher to show up on time or to come prepared or to embrace a solutions-oriented mindset because the structure and the relationship are so broken. He feels like asking these things would be like someone trying to make the beds on a sinking cruise ship. It's not going to help! I need to get out of here!

Have you ever been Ray? Even just a little bit? Yeah, me too. It happens because we didn't first set expectations and then hold people accountable for meeting them.

But there's good news. Setting expectations is very doable. Even if you're midway through a coaching cycle or the school year as a whole. Even if it feels like it's too late and that you should just wait until next year. You can simply name that you're making some shifts to allow for more productivity. You can name that *you* haven't done a great job setting expectations and that, now, you are. As long as the things you share are framed as things that (a) will positively impact students and (b) are *your* misses (for not naming that these things are important) and not the teams' misses, they will likely land positively.

And please don't fall into the trap that many leaders fall into. The trap of "They should know." Yes, your teachers should know that they need to get to work on time. Or that they should submit lesson plans on time. Or that they shouldn't gossip about students or each other. They should know to dress professionally and to be prepared with fresh and engaging materials for students every day.

But that mindset doesn't help you make the things I just named happen if they're not happening. All it does is lead to frustration, resentment, and disinvestment. Leaders can start to believe they're working with a bunch of unfeeling dummies who don't care about students, because the things the leader thinks should be *obvious* are seemingly only obvious to them.

People need expectations. Without them, we can tend to go rogue. Recently, I was on line to catch a train from Philadelphia to New York. The train was late but would be arriving in five minutes. We stood there, single file and calm, waiting for our train to be called. We were following the expectations. All of us, working as a team. But then, for whatever reason, an automated voice came over the loudspeaker and announced that our train was *leaving*. That it was the *last boarding call* for us. People began to scramble. I got pushed from behind as dozens of people from the back of the line raced forward to avoid missing a train that hadn't even arrived yet. I expected someone to come onto the loudspeaker to correct this, but no one did. I expected someone to tell us what to do, but no one did. So, instead, a mob of people (of which I was one) pushed toward the escalator and the terrified gate agent. Then someone yanked back the nylon strap that blocked our path, and we all went running down the steps, panting and pushing and arriving on a quiet platform without a train in sight (I should mention here that there was another train that would be arriving in twenty minutes, so there was zero need to panic anyway).

The above is what I often see playing out in schools. Because expectations are unclear or confusing or nonexistent, people do whatever they need to in a given situation to survive. A parent comes in yelling at me, so I yell back. Because no one has ever said, despite it seeming *really* obvious, "We don't do that here." I hear students roughhousing in the hallway during a transition. But I don't step out into my doorway, because again, no one ever said, "That's the expectation."

These examples are whole-school expectations. Which I do suggest you set for the adults in your building. However, specific to coaching teachers, here are a few examples of pre-meeting expectations that you can set:

1. Always arrive on time.
2. If you're going to be late, email or text me as soon as you know, and include when I can expect you.
3. If you need to reschedule, email me 24 hours in advance.
4. Always bring your Skyrocket framework.
5. Always come prepared with the previous meeting's deliverable.

Here are some expectations you can set for a meeting:
1. No phones or tech.
2. Ten-rep rule (this pertains to setting the expectation in every meeting that you're going to have the teacher practice at least ten times).
3. No students in the room.
4. All invites on calendars.
5. Be solutions oriented.
6. No gossip.

People will often ask about food during meetings and whether it's okay if the teacher eats. One of the reasons our meetings are twenty-two minutes and not longer, is so teachers have some personal time either before or after the meeting to eat, make a phone call, check emails, etc. However, not every school schedule is the same, and if your teacher is hungry, you *should* invite them to eat. Hungry people can be everything from angry to distracted, and you don't want either one sitting across from you.

Here are some expectations you can set for after the meeting:
1. Email responses within 48 hours.
2. All deliverables submitted on time.
3. If you can't meet a deadline, please email me before the deadline with a new deadline.
4. Email me if you need *anything*.

To be clear, you won't choose all of the above. But choose (or design) the ones that resonate the most. First, ask the teacher what they'll need from *you* to be successful. Then share your four or five expectations. Ask them to write them down. Thank them when they meet them. "Hey, thanks for being prepared for our session. Let's get started." And address it when they don't. "You're five minutes late and I didn't get a text. What's going on and how can I support you in meeting this expectation going forward?"

It may feel weird at first, but once you normalize it, it'll feel weird *not* to do it.

Ultimately, I invite you to see accountability less as a place to share what someone did "wrong" and more as an opportunity to support them. Years ago, an assistant principal I knew referred to accountability as a handshake. She said, "I share what I expect of my team, and whether we physically shake hands on it or not, we *do agree* that those things are going to happen. So, when they don't, we're all able to hold each other accountable because, again, we *agreed* on them. We're able to ask, 'What happened? Why weren't you able to do the thing we all agreed we'd do? How can I support you on it in the future?'"

Oftentimes, educators think that they need to have authority over someone to hold them accountable. And that the way to hold someone accountable is through write-ups and memos. But that's simply untrue. Yes, to give someone a consequence, you may need to be their manager and you may need documentation. But I'm not talking about consequences here. I'm talking about accountability. About setting an expectation, and then asking the person (or people) on the other side of that expectation to meet it.

In fact, some of the most effective coaches I work with are instructional coaches who don't directly manage their teachers. They don't have any authority over them at all. Maybe they're so good because they have to communicate so effectively and can't rely on write-ups. I'm not sure. Either way, to be an effective coach and school leader, you must be able to set expectations and then hold people accountable for meeting them. Otherwise, you risk being on the receiving end of missed meetings, late submissions, and lack of buy-in.

Set crystal-clear expectations and then hold people accountable for meeting them. And make sure you meet the expectations you set for yourself as well.

10

TWENTY-TWO-MINUTE MEETING EXECUTION

When leaders know how to lead great meetings, there's less time wasted and less frustration. We have more energy to do the work that matters, realize our full potential, and do great things.
—Justin Rosenstein

Our coaching meetings are twenty-two minutes long. That's a relatively short meeting in the world of education. There are two reasons why. The first is because teachers are busy. And as we discussed earlier, you shouldn't apologize or undermine yourself because they're busy. But they *are* busy. So, a twenty-two-minute meeting allows most teachers to eat something, meet with you, and then use the bathroom before their students return. The second reason is that a twenty-two-minute meeting *forces you* to be uber-prepared. I've observed hundreds of thirty-minute, forty-minute, and even fifty-minute meetings that could have been half as long had the coach been prepared, had an agenda, had clear outcomes, etc. Ours is a fast meeting partly because in a fast meeting, *you* have to be at your *very best* the entire time. Think of it this way: If you're running five miles, a few missteps won't make a ton of difference in your overall time. But if you're running a hundred-meter sprint, those missteps could be the difference between first place and last.

Below are our coaching meeting's six components, along with detailed descriptions of them and their suggested lengths. As a note, some of these components were discussed in the chapter on preparation. That was about their design, whereas what follows is about how to deliver them.

CHECK-IN/AGENDA

Begin every meeting by thanking the teacher for being there (remember not to undermine yourself by saying things like "This will be quick" or "I know you're really busy.") Then check in with the teacher. Try to make this something personal versus something school related. You're about to talk school for twenty or so minutes, so asking about their daughter's soccer tournament over, for instance, how third period is going will help you continue to build a trusting and friendly relationship. Also, third period might not be going that well, and while that's definitely something you'll want to know about, now is not the time. You can't afford to spend ten minutes talking about third period, all while derailing your entire meeting. To that point, keep this check-in short, as there's a lot to cover in the meeting. Far too many coaching meetings begin with three to five minutes (or more) of fluff. This may be nice, but it's not going to help the teacher get better.

Next, name what's going to happen in the meeting. Teachers like details and they *hate* surprises, so letting them know exactly what's going to happen can help set both of you up for success, as they'll know exactly what to expect. Your language can sound something like this:

> So, let me share what we're going to do today. First, I'm going to share a glow from this week. This is something

you're doing really effectively that's having a positive impact on students that you'll want to continue. Next, I'll share a grow. This is the thing we're going to spend our time working on to further impact student outcomes. After that, we'll practice for fifteen minutes. Then we'll set some really rigorous but attainable goals for you and the students. And finally, we'll close by talking about next steps.

This is also the point at which you'll ask if the teacher has brought whatever you needed him to bring to be successful in that meeting. This should definitely include his Skyrocket framework. Beyond that, it should include whatever you've asked him to prepare for that meeting, like scripted directions, this week's lesson plans, higher-order questions, etc. It's important that you set the expectation that teachers are coming to your meetings to work. It's always a red flag for me when I'm observing a coaching session and the teacher arrives without any deliverables or anything to write on or write with. This means the coach hasn't set these as expectations.

If the teacher doesn't have what you've asked them to bring, you should ask them to go get it. Yes, you'll lose meeting time, but what time you do have will be more productive. Also, make sure you remind them of the expectation of arriving with what was asked so you can maximize the time in upcoming meetings. If the teacher simply didn't create the thing you needed them to create, think about rescheduling the meeting. This is not ideal, but slogging through a meeting where one party is unprepared likely won't be the best use of your time. Again, remind them of the expectation of arriving prepared. And in this case, set (or reset) the expectation that they should email you beforehand if they've been unable to complete what you've asked.

This part of the meeting, with the check-in and the agenda-share, should last one minute.

GLOW

Share one or two things the teacher is doing well *and* how it's impacting student outcomes. Try to make this something you recently worked on (ideally from the last meeting). This allows for the teacher to see how their work on skill X is really paying off. Even if this glow isn't their *biggest* glow, sharing something you just worked on also helps contribute to you and the teacher reinforcing shared language. Ensure that the glow is replete with data, including student names, time stamps, and direct quotes from students and the teacher.

At the end of the data-share, ask the teacher to reflect. You can say something more general like, "So what do you think about that?" However, if you're working with a teacher who is more hesitant to share, you may want to ask more pointed questions that force the teacher to reflect: "What one thing about that data stands out to you most?," "What are the two things you're most proud of about what I shared?"

This part of the meeting should last two minutes.

GROW

It is important that as you're shifting from the glow to the grow, that you don't change your tone. The grow is not *bad*. It's simply the current biggest lever for increasing student outcomes. The data you've collected around it is unbiased and together, you and the teacher are going to work on it. Again, use student names, time stamps, and direct quotes from students and the teacher. And then share what teacher action is going to move the needle.

At this point, ask the teacher to reflect on what you've shared. It's *very* important that you ask the teacher to reflect *after* you've shared the teacher action you're going to work on. Otherwise, you could run the risk of the teacher reactively looking for excuses, as they may feel challenged or confronted (which is not the goal).

See this nonexample:

> Four of twenty-three students were on task during the do now. James and Tanya were yelling at each other at 9:08. Christian was walking around the room from 9:09 until 9:14. And May and Jansen were sleeping. What are your thoughts on that?

A teacher hearing this may feel threatened and, whether he believes it or not, try to put this on their kids:

> Well, May and Jansen don't do anything in any class. And James and Tanya have been fighting for weeks.

And so on. None of these things are helpful at all.

Compare that with this:

> Four of twenty-three students were on task during the do now. James and Tanya were yelling at each other at 9:08. And May and Jansen were sleeping. We're going to focus on building a really solid routine for starting that do now, which I'm confident will result in more on-task behavior. What are your thoughts on that?

Here, you're presenting the data as fact. Which it is. The reflection is on the teacher action you're going to work on and not on the student behavior. This will lead to the teacher reflecting on the solution you're providing versus potentially feeling challenged by data that might be upsetting.

This part of the meeting should last two minutes.

PRACTICE

This is the most important part of the meeting. It should begin with you naming the criteria for excellence and then modeling that criteria. Sometimes multiple times. The teacher needs to see what the steps for success looks like in order to begin to build this habit. But to see those steps, you as the coach need to be able to name them.

Remember that you must be able to name *what makes the thing the thing*. As smart and talented as your teachers are, it's simply not enough to tell a teacher she needs to praise more, and then ask her to do that without clear criteria for success.

That criteria needs to be presented to the teacher here and then named. Too often, coaches model (which is a win), but don't name the criteria. Sometimes they even say, "What did you notice?" hoping the teacher will land on it herself. Again, this is not a good use of time, as the time here should be spent practicing, not guessing about what makes the thing the thing.

Look at this example script you could use for Strand One:

> So, we're going to dive into positive praise right here. Before we do, I'd like to talk through our criteria. The first thing we're going to do is ensure we always say the student's name whom we're praising. The second thing we're going to do is we're going to name the exact behavior the student is engaging in. And finally, we're going to make eye contact with that student. So instead of, "Nice job, everyone," we'd say, "John, thank you for sharing your response with your neighbor," all while looking at John. Does that make sense? Do you have any questions before I model? Great!

Then you would stand up and model a few times, before asking the teacher to dive in.

Look at this example script you could use for Strand Two:

> We're going to design lesson hooks, which is 2.5. Before we start scripting, I want to share my criteria. The first thing is that a lesson hook should be under two minutes long. Next, it shouldn't be school related. Video clips, a portion of a song they like, sports highlights, or an article all work. Finally, students must have an observable task during the hook. Does that make sense? Do you have any questions before I share my model?

A few additional notes here: First, make sure you frame practice as something beneficial. Or at the very least, don't undermine yourself by sarcastically saying something like, "Now it's time for the *fun part*," or "Now it's time for your *favorite thing*." The teacher needs to get better at X so that students can do better at Y. It's that simple. Yes, practicing and scripting in front of another adult can be awkward at first. What's decidedly more awkward is having to explain to parents that the reason their child didn't get the best education possible is because you didn't want to feel uncomfortable in a coaching meeting. Also, while practicing can often be awkward at first, usually after a few reps, teachers (because many teachers are *really* competitive) will start insisting they do more, saying things like "Let me do that again" or "I can do that better."

Next, when the teacher is practicing (particularly during a get-up-and-say-it practice), stand next to her. Show her you're in this together and that she's not performing for you as you sit at a desk watching. Also, standing next to her allows you to more actively provide feedback while she's practicing. You can also more easily interject when a certain rep doesn't meet the bar: "That was good, but you're missing one piece. Let me do another one so you can watch my body language. Okay, your turn."

And finally, whatever you do, don't play a student. There's no bigger waste of your skill and expertise than for you to pretend you're an eight-year-old. You can imagine there's an eight-year-old in front of you while you stand next to your teacher, coaching him along the way.

Shoot for as many reps as you can get in fifteen minutes. And don't stop when she's gotten one or two good ones. Go ten or fifteen reps beyond that so you can get to the place of automaticity. Remember, the goal here is that the teacher gets significantly better at whatever skill you're working on, that she builds a habit so that she can do the thing and do it really well when it matters most: when she's in front of students. So push for as many great reps as you can get in the time allotted.

One note here is that it's more difficult to get in a lot of reps when you're practicing Strand Two or Strand Three skills. With something like clear directions (1.7), you can get upwards of twenty or thirty reps pretty easily. But, likely, you won't have time for a teacher to script twenty or thirty objectives (2.1), for instance, in one session. Don't let this obstacle change your approach. You should still provide the teacher with a model and clearly name the criteria. Then have her practice repeatedly, all while giving feedback. It'll look different, as you'll be both be sitting and there will be a lot of silent time as she's writing. But she should present an objective to you after you've modeled and she's scripted, and you should provide feedback on that objective. Then have her do another. And then provide feedback. If it seems like she's really getting it, have her do two or three more at once and review them all at the same time.

This part of the meeting should take fifteen minutes.

GOALS

As we discussed in chapter seven, it's immensely important to create goals in your coaching relationships. At this point in the meeting, you should share both a teacher goal and a student outcome goal with the teacher. What's important here is that the teacher is very aware of these goals. Let's say the teacher goal is that every direction includes time, task, materials, and sound (1.7), and the student goal is that 85 percent of students follow all parts of the direction within fifteen seconds of the teacher giving it. You'll share these goals with the teacher,

get their feedback, and then let them know you'll be tracking this in the class. All your data collected should be around progress toward *these* goals.

This part of the meeting should take one minute.

NEXT STEPS

The meeting should end with the three next steps you planned into your agenda. The first is putting the next meeting on the calendar. And by on the calendar, I mean you should have your computer open and send the invite right then. Perhaps you and the teacher have standing meetings, and this is fine too. Then this is the time to reconfirm this next meeting. The next piece is your next observation. And again, this should be put on your calendars. You may have a standing observation time as well, but unlike the standing meeting, which is a fine idea, a standing observation time means you always see the teacher with the same students, on the same day, and at the same time of day. This can lead to the collection of corrupt data that may not paint a full enough picture of what's happening in the teacher's classroom. Put one scheduled observation on the calendar, while also letting teachers know that you'll be in at multiple other points.

Finally, make sure you share the deliverable you planned. This is the thing that the teacher needs to produce and send to you before your next meeting. If you scripted out routines for entering the classroom, moving from the chairs to the rug, and responding to teacher questions using choral responses, have the teacher email you scripted routines for students handing in homework and exiting the classroom. If you scripted out a week's worth of objectives, have them script out next week's objectives and send them your way. Maybe it's not scripting, but you want them to observe and write a reflection after seeing a teacher who has students respond to each other using academic language. Maybe they watch video of their own class, and then send you a reflection on that.

To be clear, this task has to be impactful or you risk disinvesting the teacher. But if the task is impactful, you allow for learning to continue, even though you're not directly working with the teacher. Like the personal trainer I referenced earlier, many coaching relationships exist *only* in the handful of minutes per week that a coach and teacher see each other. This can hinder progress and, in a worst-case scenario, train teachers to simply tolerate their time with you, as it'll be over quickly, and they won't be accountable for anything after the meeting.

This deliverable should be put on the calendar and you should insist on specificity around submission times. The "end of the day on Thursday" might mean 4 p.m. It might mean 5 p.m. It might mean midnight. Insist on clarity and then send an email invite with the task and the time. Then thank the teacher for their time and effort in the meeting.

This part of the meeting should take one minute.

Finally, make sure not to default to what most co-planning meetings look like. In these meetings, a teacher and a coach plan one lesson from top to bottom. They find the materials and resources together, design the do now as a team, then they create the direct instruction, and so on. What happens here is that *one* really solid lesson is created. But what also happens is that the teacher doesn't get radically better at anything. So, after that lesson is taught, the teacher isn't prepared to design the next one on his own.

To use a real-life example here, if I wanted to learn how to build a house and you were an expert homebuilder, it wouldn't be all that helpful for you to show me all the different aspects of building *one* house in one shot. If you brought me along as the builders laid the concrete and then erected the 2x4s for the walls and then nailed up the sheetrock and so on, I wouldn't actually *learn* how to build a house. I'd have a *sense* of how to build a house. Just like the previous teacher would have a sense of how to design a really effective lesson. What would be *more effective*, however, would be for you to take me to one house and show me how to pour the concrete for the foundation. Then, you'd take me to another house, and I'd watch you do that again. By house three, I'd be doing it with your support. By houses four and five I'd be doing it mostly solo. And on and on until I was an expert at that one part. Then the next day we'd move on to the next step. And you'd train me to become an expert at that. It may seem like this approach takes longer, but I'd argue that the first approach is ineffective when to comes to building habits—which is why coaches who go this route are often working on general lesson design with their teachers all year long.

Focus on one thing. Master it. Then move on.

PART FOUR:
ORBIT

11
REAL-TIME-COACHING (RTC) MINDSET

In a growth mindset, challenges are exciting rather than threatening. So rather than thinking, "Oh, I'm going to reveal my weaknesses," you say, "Wow, here's a chance to grow."
—Carol Dweck

After a meeting, it's time to provide ongoing support to your teachers. The most effective way to do that is through real-time coaching. Those words often send chills down the spines of coaches and teachers alike. If you're unfamiliar with the term, it refers to the act of a school leader providing coaching to her teachers *while* they're teaching. It can often look like the coach entering the room while the teacher is instructing, and then, using predetermined signals or verbal cues, providing coaching to the teacher in real time, based on what's happening in the room.

Real-time coaching should be focused on *driving student outcomes* through specific and targeted feedback on bite-sized actions that will move the needle in the room. For example, if the baseline data says that 65 percent of the students in the class are on task, and you determine that redirection will *increase* students on task, your real-time coaching should be focused on building this skill (after the teacher has had training on it) through real-time coaching strategies. You will provide real-time coaching intentionally and strategically to prompt the teacher to provide redirection whenever redirection is not occurring, all while you collect data on what the on-task percentage is when the teacher *isn't* redirecting versus when he *is*.

This kind of coaching has an *immediate* impact on teacher practice and student learning versus the coaching meeting that occurs later that day or later that week. While these meetings will be impactful, by the time they happen, the teacher may have taught a handful (or dozens) of lessons with that same area of improvement not having been addressed.

What can often make real-time coaching difficult for coaches, at least initially, is the concern over how real-time coaching will be received by staff (and sometimes by students). I remember the first time I was asked to provide real-time coaching to teachers, I was sick to my stomach. I imagine some folks reading this now are feeling similarly. That's okay. And some of the rationale I had for why RTC was a bad idea is the same as what many school leaders share about it when I meet with them now.

Here's the transcript of a friendly conversation I recently had with a principal who said he didn't want to provide real-time coaching for his teachers. He didn't want to offend them. They're professionals after all. Real-time coaching could be demeaning. He reminded me a lot of myself early on.

Me: "Do you have children of your own?"
Coach: "Yes. Two girls."
Me: "How would you feel if they weren't getting the best education they could possibly get?"
Coach: "I'd be upset about that. Obviously."
Me: "What if you found out that the person *whose job* it is to make sure your daughters are getting the *best education possible* wasn't doing *everything* he could do to ensure that?"
Coach: "Yeah, I get it. I'd definitely be annoyed by that."
Me: "That instead of thinking about your daughters, he was thinking about himself and the other adults first. He believes your

daughters' teachers just need to just figure it out. Even if that means they get a worse education as a result. Maybe they lose an entire year of instruction. Maybe it affects them the rest of their lives, as they're never able to catch up. To be clear, the coach knows what to do. And he agrees it would be beneficial. He's simply uncomfortable doing it. He's concerned about the response he may get."

Coach: "Okay. Okay, yes [*laughing*]. I'd be down at the school. Likely screaming for somebody's head."

Me: "[*Laughing*] You should be. Are you ready to change your approach now?"

Coach: "Yes."

This coach flipped his mindset pretty easily. That's great. But others need more than a mindset shift. They want ideas on framing, different approaches, and different techniques to get on board. Here are *some* arguments against RTC, along with some counterpoints designed to support you in feeling as comfortable as possible with diving headfirst into RTC:

"I don't want to undermine the teacher."

If a teacher is struggling, he's already undermined. Nobody in the room, whether they're five or fifteen, believes things are going well. And forcing him to struggle more, to the detriment of the students in the class, is really unfair to everyone.

"I don't want to interrupt the lesson."

If the teacher is really struggling (like the previous teacher), then what's the concern? That we'd be interrupting students who are talking when they should be working, who are walking around when they should be sitting, who are potentially arguing with each other all while the teacher tries in vain to get them back on task? That lesson *needs* to be interrupted.

If the lesson is going okay, but there are opportunities to engage more students or provide more clarity, then "interrupting" will actually lead to more students understanding the material. And we *should* step in when that's the case. Because it's what's best for kids.

In addition, and this is from a former administrator of mine, the second you walk into a room, you've interrupted the lesson. Everyone becomes aware of you and your presence. The simple act of speaking alone doesn't do this.

"What will students think?"

Students are really smart. *And* they also don't care that much. If framed well (I discuss this later in the chapter), kids get on board very quickly with another adult asking questions and providing support in the room.

"What if my coaching doesn't change things? What if I'm not skilled enough to coach effectively?"

You have your job for a reason. Because you're a talented educator. While every last piece of coaching you provide may not have the desired impact, you should feel confident (particularly after reading this book) that (a) you've chosen the right thing to work on (or close to it), and (b) your relationships with your teachers are strong enough that you can sometimes miss the mark and it won't damage your ability to coach them going forward.

There are about a dozen other reasons *not* to provide real-time coaching. Many of which may make sense in a vacuum. But many of which are about our concerns about not being able to get everyone (teachers *and* students) bought in to us and this approach. To be clear, the school leaders I speak with believe real-time coaching is effective. They believe their teachers and students deserve it. But the teachers and students aren't what's stopping them. It's their own insecurities.

If you find yourself thinking about all the reasons why real-time coaching will be uncomfortable and challenging for you, I encourage you to shift your thinking away from what *you want* and what *you're feeling*, to what is best for your students and your schools.

Start slowly if you need to. Be okay with your real-time coaching being clunky early on. Because even if it's less than wholly effective at the start, you'll build your confidence, as well as normalize this process for teachers and students. Yes, initially, you'll probably coach like the person who drops a ring into the sink and has to fish it out of the garbage disposal. Even though the disposal's turned off, you slide your hand in quickly, finding the thing you need, and yanking it out, breathing heavily, feeling like you barely escaped from something terrible happening. You'll give a little bit of feedback, your heart racing as you do, and quickly retreat to the back of the room. Soon it'll became more comfortable, and eventually it'll became second nature. But it starts with you potentially changing what *you believe* about real-time coaching.

A note here around the use of headsets and earpieces to provide real-time coaching: This is a strategy we've observed but do not use for multiple reasons. First, we find the technology cumbersome. Simply put, sometimes it doesn't work. And valuable coaching is missed out upon because of it. Most of the time, though, it does work. However, it can be distracting as the teacher is trying to instruct, and instead of the coach providing a noticeable and agreed upon pause point to give feedback in person (as described earlier in the chapter), the teacher is asked to process feedback from his coach while students, unaware he has an earpiece in, stare at him, wondering why he stopped speaking or changed course. This doesn't always happen, of course. And this kind of coaching can be impactful. However, often, because the coach is not in the room and not visible, the feedback to the teacher is ignored and needs to be followed up on later.

One final point here is that when asked, school teams often share that they use headsets and earpieces as a strategy to minimize the potential awkwardness and distraction of providing real-time coaching. The students don't know, the teacher doesn't feel undermined, etc. This to me is a backdoor attempt at solving a "problem" that can be solved more easily on the front end through relationships, framing, and transparency with everyone involved.

Below are a few best practices for getting started with real-time coaching and for sharing it with your staff. Because often, the reason why we walk out of rooms, and away from teachers and students who could use our support, is because we haven't framed real-time coaching in a way that causes the staff to the embrace the idea versus bristling at it.

- Real-time coaching should be presented to teachers as support and *not* something punitive. Language that sounds like "This is something I'm going to be providing for everyone in an effort to further support you and your students" is more likely to get buy-in than something that sounds like "So, if you're not giving clear directions, I'll step in and correct you." While the latter may technically be true, this kind of framing may leave teachers feeling nervous about each visit, whereas the former could leave them excited to grow.

- Teachers should know that you'll interject in the least invasive way possible. While you are the boss/superior and likely don't *need* to do this, saying, "Excuse me, Ms. Smith, can I interject for a moment?" goes a long way toward ensuring the teacher feels comfortable with this support. The same end goal is achieved, and the teacher is empowered in the process.

- Real-time coaching should be messaged to students. This can happen with individual classes or with entire grades. You can share a version of the following with students:

I want to let you know about a shift we're making this year. In order to provide you with the most support possible, you're going to see me in your classes, asking you questions, talking about what you're working on, and providing feedback for your teachers, sometimes while they're teaching you. I've told your teachers about this, and they're excited about it. You should know that this isn't a punishment or anything negative at all. It's simply another opportunity for me to get to work with you all.

You can also use this rollout to model for students what this will look like. You may even ask a teacher to join you in front of the room. You can model a few different scenarios like the ones below:
- "Ms. James, can I interject for a moment? Can you ask all students to write a response here?"

- "Mr. Lee, can I step in to ask you to please remind students of the sound expectation?"

- "Ms. Sullivan, let's have students share their responses with their neighbors."

The frame is of immense importance, but of equal importance are the techniques themselves.

12

REAL-TIME COACHING TECHNIQUES

Strive for continuous improvement, instead of perfection.
—Kim Collins

At Skyrocket, we use four different real-time-coaching techniques to coach teachers. While some are more effective for different situations, each school leader should choose the technique or techniques she's most comfortable with and norm with teachers on what they are and when they'll be used.

They're provided below in order from least invasive to most invasive.

SIGNALING

Signaling is the least invasive of the RTC techniques we employ. It involves the coach signaling to the teacher, and the teacher responding by making the shift the signal is prompting him toward. If the teacher misses providing students with a time limit in his directions, you can point at your watch (or wrist). If there's an opportunity for all students to engage in writing, you can mime the motion of a moving pencil. The simpler the gesture the better, as you don't want to look like a first base coach out there. I've done this. I've seen this. It doesn't go well.

Signaling only works, however, when you and the teacher have previously agreed upon a signal, practiced the signal in isolation, and agreed upon the teacher's response after the signal is given.

During signaling, you'll usually stand in the back of the room, facing the teacher, so he can see you easily. And while real-time coaching shouldn't be hidden from students, the signals you provide *are* often missed by the students. This makes signaling a great place to start for a coach and teacher who are just beginning this process.

WHISPERING

Whisper coaching, while more invasive than signaling, is often a favorite of newer coaches and more hesitant teachers. With whisper coaching, you'll step up to the teacher and whisper a question, a direction, a request to praise students, an invitation to check for understanding together, etc. While the students will likely notice this (think back to the importance of framing here), and the momentum of the class will stop momentarily, the act of whispering gives both you and the teacher the ability to pause for a moment to communicate privately. Again, a prompt needs to be agreed upon in advance for the sake of both speed and clarity.

- Nonexample: "Hey, I noticed you asked that question and then asked for volunteers. I think this would be a super opportunity for you to ask all students to write. What do you think?"

- Example: "Let's have all students write here."

- Example: "Can we have all students write here?"

- Example: "Everybody writes."

One key to making whisper coaching effective is ensuring that you are in close enough proximity to the teacher while she's instructing to be able to whisper to her when the moment arises. Opportunities to provide feedback can be missed if you're too far away and the teacher has already moved on to something else.

QUESTIONING

Questioning is an invasive technique, but it's a favorite of many coaches and teachers as it's usually seen as gentle and empowering by everyone involved. After the teacher gives a direction or a task for students, you will question the teacher, using a predetermined and agreed-upon questioning technique, which prompts the teacher to respond back to students with an additional task, direction, or request (responding to students is key—if the teacher simply responds back to you, there was likely a miss in your practice of this technique).

Example 1:
Teacher: "Okay students, please take out your notebooks and silently copy down today's objective."
Coach: "Excuse me, Mr. Flynn. How long do students have to do this?"
Teacher: "Students, please take thirty seconds to do this."

Example 2:
Teacher: "Who can tell me what we learned yesterday?"

Coach: "Ms. Rodriguez, can we have all students write a response here?"

Teacher: "Yes, that's a great idea. Everyone please write down two things you learned in yesterday's lesson."

MODELING

The last technique is called modeling and it's by far the most invasive of the four. Modeling is largely reserved for the coach and teacher who have a rock-solid rapport and who are both all in on coaching, or for the coach working with a teacher who is struggling so mightily that the other three techniques won't move the room quickly enough. Modeling is when you engage in the *exact behavior* you want the *teacher* to engage in, which then sparks the teacher to follow.

Example 1:

Teacher: "Students, when I say 'go,' please take one minute to answer questions three through eight."

Coach: "I see James has already begun working silently. Thank you, James. I see Tanya has begun working silently as well. Thanks, Tanya."

Teacher: "I also see Melanie and Jayden and have begun working silently. Thank you, both."

Example 2:

Teacher: "Everyone please turn to your neighbor and share your thoughts about the prompt on the board."

Coach: "Ms. Polk, let's have all students generate a response first before sharing with partners."

Teacher: "Sounds good. Students, please take one minute to generate a response to the prompt on the board. After one minute, we'll share those responses with our partners."

CLOSING THOUGHTS ON REAL-TIME COACHING

Recently, a school leader shared with me his hesitance to provide real-time coaching for his teachers. His belief was that his presence in the room would change the students' actions. He believed that *he* could get them to understand the content more deeply because of his years of teaching experience and his content expertise. And he believed that *he* could have them engage in more on-task behavior because of his strength of relationships, strong presence, and myriad engagement strategies (his title of principal would likely help as well). However, he worried about his teachers' ability to do the same once he left. *He'd* see everything that was missing and be able to fix it in a few minutes, but would his teacher then be set up for success? This is a valid concern, but one that illustrates some potential misconceptions around real-time coaching. I list two of these misconceptions and elaborate on them here.

> *Misconception 1: Real-time coaching can and should be provided for anything the coach observes. It should be about fixing everything that's missing, every time the coach enters the room.*

In fact, it's just the opposite. Real-time coaching should be focused on the particular skill you're working on. Real-time coaching is often unsuccessful because the coach sees something in the moment and gives feedback on it. But what if what the leader saw is not something the coach and the teacher ever discussed, so the teacher doesn't know what to do to address it. We call this *Wild, Wild West coaching*. In the Wild West, there weren't a lot of rules, and people pretty much did whatever they wanted. It was unpredictable and likely stressful. Wild, Wild West coaching feels like this to teachers.

This coaching usually occurs as whisper coaching and it sounds like "Try to engage more kids," or "Make sure to check their work." But without modeling, practicing to build a skill, and an agreement on which RTC technique the coach will use, this kind of coaching can do more harm than good. It leaves teachers skittish when their coaches enter the room, as they're unsure of what they'll receive feedback on. And because the feedback is random and the teacher doesn't have the model and the practice session(s) to pull from, no skill is built. No habits are reinforced. Maybe something changes in the moment, but when the coach leaves, that change usually does too.

This is tough for some coaches, because it means they'll need to pace themselves and be okay with something not being great as they work on the agreed-upon skill. This may be misperceived as a lowering of the bar. If we put students first and we do whatever it takes to be great for them, then why should a coach ignore something that they can support the teacher on? The answer is because people don't build skill by working on a lot of seemingly random things at once, without training, and without a clear model of what success looks like. A temporary change is not worth the teacher frustration, the time lost on the skill they're currently working on, and the potential damage to the relationship.

If you and your teacher are working on directions but the teacher could also use coaching on praise, the praise waits. If you're working on stating the objective but the teacher's model is too long, the model must wait. And so on. Because real-time coaching should *always* be focused on building teacher skill and not simply fixing something that's happening in a particular observation.

This holds true in all but two cases. The first is if what's happening in the class is dangerous. In this instance, do whatever it takes to support the teacher. Then coach him like crazy so his class isn't ever dangerous again. The second is if the teacher is being unkind to students. If his language is sarcastic, offensive, or downright cruel, pull the teacher aside, name what's happening, ask if everything is okay, and then tell him to stop it.

Misconception 2: This is an opportunity for school leaders to do what they do best: engage with students.

This, too, is untrue. You're likely great at engaging students. Which is probably part of the reason why you were promoted in the first place. But using your personality or rapport or overall presence to effect change more quickly in the room, while likely making an immediate impact, might hurt the teacher long-term.

Years ago, I was working with a school leader from one of the largest school districts in the country. It was early on in our relationship, so I was shadowing her to determine glow and grow areas. In the first classroom we entered, the teacher was instructing about fifteen students at the front of the room, while eight other students were joking around in the back of the room. They were standing around, talking, and laughing like they were at a school dance and not in class. It was *mostly* playful, but concerning, nonetheless.

Immediately, the school leader snapped her fingers and yelled to the students in the back, "Hey! Sit down *right* now!" And all eight students did.

The teacher meekly thanked her boss, barely making eye contact afterward. As we exited the room, the school leader seemed very proud of her ability to be able to get students to sit down, as she said, "Kids here listen to me."

My response was the following: "Got it. But how did what you just did help the teacher get better?"

She couldn't answer. And shortly thereafter, on my suggestion, we walked back by that same class and saw the same eight students standing in the back of the room, except now they were talking even louder, potentially *more* emboldened. It was then she realized that she hadn't helped the teacher at all. She'd been well-intentioned but had likely made the teacher's job harder, as everyone in that room was now aware, *especially* the teacher, that the school leader was able to do in five seconds what the teacher hadn't been able to do all year. And those eight students, likely knowing the school leader wouldn't be back that period, took advantage of the situation. This school leader, in doing what she did best, risked leaving the teacher feeling hopeless. Because it was so easy for the leader. Because it was so natural. But that teacher needed a coach, not a bouncer.

She needed skill-building, not a quick fix. She needed to be trained, not to be saved.

The days of a principal handing a new teacher their classroom keys and a bunch of books and saying, "Have a nice career. I'll see you in thirty years," are long gone. The sitting-in-the-back-of-the-room-typing-and-emailing-feedback-three-days-later model of coaching leaves too much time between the lesson and the learning, and by then, the teacher may have forgotten what was even happening in that class. Real-time coaching can be intense. It can be uncomfortable at first. But it's also a key lever that leaders can pull so everyone in the building can continue to improve for students.

PART FIVE:
LANDING

13
BEST PRACTICES

There isn't enough time to manage people. What is the reality? Since your time is so limited, you definitely don't have time to deal with all the things that go wrong when you do not spend enough time up front managing people. When you spend your time managing, you engage the productive capacity of the people you manage and improve the quality and output of the employee's work for hours or days. That's a good return on investment.
—Bruce Tulgan

About fifteen years ago, I was invited to a bachelor party. Twenty men, renting a house for the weekend by the beach on Long Island, cooking, playing volleyball, maybe indulging in an adult beverage or two, and sending our buddy into the world of marriage in style.

One of the men invited was a friend of a friend. I'd never met him before. He was a personal trainer who had the best physique I'd ever seen on a human being in my life. In fact, he was so serious about his fitness that he brought kettlebells to the party. If you don't know what kettlebells are, just know that they're used for working out, and that it's totally insane to bring them to a bachelor party weekend.

At this time in my life, I was in pretty good shape too. Not as good as him, but pretty good. At one point he actually asked me what my routine was, as according to him I was "pretty ripped."

I was thrilled. Like if you were humming on an elevator and the person behind you leaned over and told you that you had a good voice. And then you saw that that person was Beyoncé!

Fast forward fifteen years to a different beach on Long Island, not far from where that bachelor party was. I saw the personal trainer for the first time since then. He was still in tip-top shape. But me, I'd put on thirty-five pounds and lost much of my muscle tone. We shook hands and he looked me up and down and said, "Dude, what happened?"

I began running through the list of all the reasons why I was no longer in good shape.

"I started my own business and that's stressful."

"I travel a lot."

"It's hard to eat well on the road."

"I had three kids."

"We have a lot of personal commitments, so it's hard to get to the gym."

"I sometimes eat the kids' leftovers."

"I'm older. My metabolism has slowed down."

I shared all the things that I'd been telling myself for why I was no longer in great shape. I'd shared these stories with *many people* in my life in the years prior to this, and through my repetition and others' acknowledgement of them being really valid reasons, they'd become "true."

But not to the trainer who looked me right in the eyes and said, "Bullsh*t."

And then he went through each excuse and dismantled them. One by one.

My favorite was when he said, *"You* didn't have three kids. Your wife did. And she looks great. And as for not having time to work out, if you watch ten minutes of TV a day, you have time to work out. Do you watch ten minutes of TV a day?"

His unbelievably direct feedback blew my world up. I'd created this forcefield of excuses as to why I couldn't do something that, in my heart, I really wanted to do. And he blew it up. So, I cut out the excuses and lost the weight in four months.

Nearly *every* school leader I meet says they don't coach effectively because they don't have the time. It's the first thing they share. It's not *their* fault. It's lack of time. They tell that to other school leaders and *those leaders* agree, and that time excuse becomes an almost impenetrable forcefield that school leaders are protected behind. And I want to blow it up. Because it's not true. It's never once been true. I don't even have to know you to know it's not true for you. Which doesn't mean that time isn't in short supply in your work. There aren't *any* school leaders who walk around saying, "Man, I *cannot believe* how much free time I have! This is amazing!" However, time is not the issue. It's lack of focus and preparation that lead to a lack of deliberateness around coaching. Once you're as focused and prepared as I'm coaching you to be, the time you have will be spent much more intentionally. Even if we don't find even one extra minute in your day, it'll feel like you have more time because you'll be more productive. That being said, I do believe we can find some more time in your schedule, while also ensuring your coaching is more intentional. Here's how.

First, don't coach everyone in your building at once. Unless your school has five teachers, coaching everyone at once is too big a lift for you to truly provide the level of support you'll need to provide to make your teachers great. Leaders who try this almost always fail. They can't keep up with the demand, and they begin missing meetings and seeing people less and less often, undermining themselves along the way. Pretty soon, coaching is this random thing that happens sometimes and doesn't happen others.

It varies for principals versus, say, an instructional coach who works with teachers all day, but Skyrocket's coaching here is to coach as many people as you can, while still being able to have five touch points per week per teacher. Yes, you read that right. Michael Phelps became the greatest Olympian of all time, not by practicing once a week, but by practicing *all the time*.

A touch point is defined in three ways:
- A coaching meeting.

- An observation (not simply collecting data, but real-time coaching too).

- An additional learning experience (such as an observation of another teacher, an article to read and reflect on, reviewing and reflecting on a video of their own class or someone else's, etc.).

The one-observation-per-week model just won't move your teachers as much as you likely need them to. Multiple observations per teacher per week can feel daunting, but since your time will be spent more strategically, multiple observations will feel much more doable. Don't feel compelled to put all these observations on the calendar either. First, you'll want to be responsive. While I never suggest canceling a meeting or an observation, as this can undermine you, having a block of time set aside each day or each week to pop into teachers' rooms will allow you to prioritize the teachers and classes who need your attention the most.

Also, you really want to build a culture of continuous learning and feedback in your building. If all your observations are scheduled, it's possible even your most bought-in teachers might put a little something extra into the lesson you're coming to see. On one hand, it's great that they'd care enough to go above and beyond on that day. But you ultimately want them to always go above and beyond, whether you're there or not. Put one scheduled observation on the calendar while also letting them know that you'll be in at multiple other points.

Let's get really granular about time here. A coaching meeting takes twenty-two minutes. Let's say each one takes thirty minutes to prep for (this will be the case initially, but it gets faster). Observations and real-time coaching should be focused. Remember, you're working on something very specific. You don't need to stay for the entire class period. You may need to see the entry or the introduction of the objective. Or maybe two higher-order questions during guided practice. You should look to hit ten minutes of active real-time coaching for each observation. And the additional learning is something that happens without your support. You'll review their reflection and email them back, but this should take no more than ten minutes.

If you follow the above time guidelines, you can have two meetings with a teacher, two observations with real-time coaching, and review one reflection, with prep included, in under two hours and fifteen minutes per teacher per week.

As you're setting up your teacher coaching matches, use that time frame to determine how many teachers will be coached by the different people on your staff. The principal may have three, while the instructional coach might have ten at any one time.

To that point, you should set up coaching cycles. We prescribe six-to-eight-week cycles. This time frame is short enough to feel urgent and long enough to allow for change to happen.

I recommend coaching your most struggling, Strand One teachers in cycle one. For cycle two, carry over any of the teachers who are still struggling in Strand One, while adding some teachers who are more solid in Strand One, as well as some who are diving into Strand Two. Cycle three should be for Strand Two and Strand Three coaching. Cycle four should be the same thing, with the exception that you may think about adding some Strand One teachers into this cycle as well. These would be teachers who are struggling but who have a huge upside. Folks who you plan to ask back. Here you can coach them to finish strong and be prepared for a solid start to the next school year.

Make your coaching schedule by the end of the day on the previous Friday (this shouldn't be hard, as you'll be creating any calendar invites in real time in your meetings with teachers). Add five-minute buffers between every single item on your calendar so you can be assured of getting everywhere on time, even if someone stops you to ask a quick question as you're in transit.

To simplify the sharing of information, create a weekly update that your coaches complete by the end of the day on Friday, which includes the people they're coaching, how many touch points they had that week, what the touch points were, what was practiced, the goals they're working on, and any corresponding data. You can even have them color-code people as red, yellow, or green. Red equals minimal progress toward goals. Yellow is some progress. Green means hitting goals. This will allow for your entire leadership team (if you have one) to be aligned around who needs the most support and who you can pull back on. To that point, while we prescribe five touch points per week, if one of your teachers is always red and another is always green, you can shift from five for one teacher and five for the other to seven and three, or eight and two. This weekly update makes these decisions easier.

Finally, and this is key (and obvious), be where you say you're going to be, or immediately communicate why you won't be and reschedule. If you adopt this model, you're going to be requesting a high level of accountability from teachers. This also means that what's expected of *you* will go up. If you ask a teacher to watch a video and write a reflection, but you don't review it, you hurt your chances that they'll do it again when you ask the next time. Being late, missing meetings, and missing deadlines and deliverables is the quickest way to undermine all the pre-work you'll have done to make coaching happen at a high level.

This goes for intentional decisions you might make as well. Don't choose checklist items over driving the instructional vision of your school. Responding to that email, while something many of us just want to get off our plates, can't take precedence over an observation. That parent who stops by to speak with you, while likely well-intentioned and in need of your time, can't get it (barring an emergency situation) at the expense of every student in the teacher's class you were about to head to. Remember that you're the instructional leader charged with making sure every student is successful. So, ask yourself if the impromptu conversation about the eighth-grade dance is worth being late for a coaching meeting.

Have scheduled office hours that you make families aware of; block out time on your calendar to review lesson plans; set up thirty minutes a day to respond to emails; insist your staff read the daily email so you don't have to field questions all day about things they should know; ensure there's a plan for culture issues that go beyond what your culture team (if you have one) can handle, to make sure you're not sitting with a student all day instead of being in classrooms; delegate things like field trips and dances to teacher leaders, and try to ensure there's someone who can own any operations issues that may arise. One of the most effective school leaders I've ever worked with once told me, "I don't need to know where the rock salt is."

The more things you can put in place to ensure you're playing offense, not defense, each day, the more *time* you'll have to focus on driving the instructional vision of your school.

14
COMMON QUESTIONS

Asking questions is the first way to begin change.
—Kubra Sait

At our trainings we discuss what we call "happy hour conversations." We ask our leaders to talk through what they believe their teachers are saying about them over a few drinks at happy hour. This is a bit of a stretch for some leaders who don't totally believe (or don't want to accept) that their teachers *are* in fact talking about them. We assure them that *they are*, and we ask them to be brutally honest about what they think they're saying.

Some believe they're using flattering adjectives, like *nice*, *friendly*, and *supportive*. Others believe they're sharing less-than-flattering terms, like *inconsistent* and *poor communicator*. What's interesting, though, is that the leaders we speak with never say "unrelenting." They never say "unstoppable for students." They never say "instructional expert" or "unwavering in the pursuit of goals."

Then we ask if they want their teachers to say those things. And across the board, leaders say, "Yes."

Ultimately, nothing you do is about receiving accolades, or about getting praise you'll never hear at a happy hour you're not at. But if there is a place for you to push yourself and your staff to be even more amazing for students, to be relentless, to be unstoppable, to be that instructional expert who is unwavering in the pursuit of goals, my hope is that this book can support you in doing that.

I have included my answers to some of the more common questions we get at our trainings and onsite at schools around the country. These topics aren't all related, but they seemed to fit nicely as a conclusion to the book.

"What should I tell my teachers about Skyrocket coaching? Should I let them all know, or start small with a handful of them?"

I'm always a fan of going big with any schoolwide initiative. In my experience, the rationale for smaller rollouts often comes back to concern over how the adults will respond versus what's best for students. However, for some of you, a smaller rollout may be the right move. Regardless of whether you choose to stand in front of fifty teachers or five, you should share the rationale for why you're diving into coaching (or diving into *this* method of coaching). I encourage you to share the simplicity of the approach, the rapid change that can occur, and the focus on student outcomes. Next, share the framework with teachers. Have them do a deep dive into it. Have them write their biggest takeaways, their glows and grows as they see them, what they're most excited about, etc. Likely, your teachers will be excited about the accessibility of the framework. And while it's impossible for me to know what you currently use to coach teachers, I'll bet our model is less dense and more usable—which teachers like.

Finally, ensure that you share what coaching will look like on a day-to-day and week-to-week basis, and name for the teachers what they can count on you for. Likely, you'll need to own some misses from the past.

Maybe missed meetings, maybe lack of follow-through on other initiatives, or maybe just a lack of direct feedback. Make sure you name that you are committing to being better at those things because teachers and students deserve it.

If you do start with a smaller focus group of teachers, it's ideal if you can get them to share their successes and their thoughts on how this feels different than past coaching with your entire staff when it's time to go whole group. This is a great way to continue to get buy-in, as teachers will see that some of their colleagues are bought-in and succeeding.

Once you dive in, provide coaching updates to the staff at meetings. "We're moving into cycle two. Our goal this trimester is to have 85 percent of students on task across the school. To get there, we're going to increase our real-time coaching frequency."

The more you reference coaching, the more comfortable people will become with it. It will just be something you do in your school.

"Can I use Skyrocket to inform my PD topics?"

Yes! Certainly. But with any professional development, the presentation itself is as important as the framing on the front end, and the follow-up and accountability afterward. Teachers often complain about one-size-fits-all, sit-and-get PD. And while that is *definitely* an issue, if school leaders provided rationale for why the PD was important and then followed up through coaching, deliverables, and deadlines, teachers would be more bought-in. Teachers want to improve for their students, but they *hate* having their time wasted. Everybody does, but teachers *especially* do, because they have one hundred human variables in front of them every day who need their attention, expertise, support, and love. So having teachers sit through PD, without providing rational for why it's relevant, while they know you'll never speak about it again, drives them crazy.

So, yes, use Skyrocket to inform PD topics. Schools all over the country are doing that. Leaders will notice that teachers default to calling on one student consistently, or they'll have one student read without a task for all the others, so they'll run a schoolwide training on 2.3. But again, they frame it well on the front end—with data and student outcomes at the heart of the framing—then they observe, coach, and track it on the back end.

"I teach special education. Is this model good for my students too?"

Okay, as a former special education teacher, a person with a master's in special education, the father of a boy with autism, and the husband of an autism not-for-profit founder who's certified in applied behavior analysis (ABA), I have very strong opinions on special education and special education students. In fact, special education services were the first thing we added to our Skyrocket menu after teacher and leader coaching.

Special education teachers likely need to be even more clear with their directions and make sure their models are even more specific and direct. So, yes! It will work. And you should use it. That being said, the Skyrocket Framework for Teacher Coaching is largely a tier 1 support. It works for the overwhelming majority of students the majority of the time. Your special education students who need differentiated supports to listen, or write, or sit, or manage their emotions, will likely still need those. However, we have seen examples of students who have cognitive delays or who are emotionally disturbed or who have oppositional defiance make huge strides in classrooms that provide more structure and more direct models, and where classroom culture is strengthened and checking for understanding happens more consistently in the moment.

"I have a lot of Strand One teachers, but not a lot of Strand Two and Strand Three teachers. Is that normal?"

I often come to schools where school leaders say about this or that teacher, "He's one of my *best* teachers."

I often respond, "Based on what?"

They say something about his "content knowledge," but then I push and say, "That means he knows his content. What makes him one of your *best* teachers?"

They say, "The kids love him!"

"Great! He's an awesome relationship builder. But what's the *evidence* that he's a great teacher?"

Ultimately, we get to a place of discussing student outcomes. Sometimes the teacher's students have demonstrated radical growth in math or ELA. But often, this teacher's student progress is the same or slightly better than the other teachers in the school. This is because the person has been branded a "great teacher," when in fact, while he's great at a bunch of things in the school, when it comes to the *actual teaching* of content, he's average.

So, yes, as you bucket your teachers and you find yourself laser focused on student outcomes, you'll likely find that some of your "best" teachers, who you may have assumed were Strand Three, are actually Strand Two or even Strand One.

Do not feel discouraged by this. This is actually a good thing to find out. It's like finding out that the strange noise your car has been making for months is actually the transmission. Sure, it's annoying and it means you have to do something immediately, but it also means you can now fix it. You can focus on building the skills those teachers need to be more effective for students. It means you can provide professional development that's totally relevant to them. Finding that none of your teachers fall into Strand Two *or* Strand Three is okay. And for those teachers who do have great relationships and serious content knowledge, their awesome ability in those places will probably mean they'll grow more quickly.

"Should I set building-wide goals around coaching?"

Yes. Look at the total number of teachers on your staff. Do initial observations in September (or the end of the previous school year, if most people are returning). Bucket teachers by strand. Then set goals for total number of teachers in Strand Two by the end of the year, total number of teachers in

Strand Three by the end of the year. Set goals around schoolwide on-task numbers and content mastery data.

Example: By January 15, overall school on-task will be greater than 90 percent.

You can even set smaller goals: weekly or monthly goals, goals around total touch points, how often you provide real-time coaching, total practice time in meetings, etc. These should be done both at the start of the school year and responsively, and should be based on observation data.

In closing, our approach is more intense than other approaches, and it likely does demand more of you and your staff than what you're currently using. The practice is deeper, the accountability is higher, and the vulnerability, for everyone, is through the roof. Which can be uncomfortable.

I invite you to step into that uncomfortable place to coach teachers where they are; to be uber-prepared going into meetings; to create models where you can name what makes the thing the thing; to have teachers practice a lot in order to build habits; to provide real-time coaching; and to make sure you're holding yourself, and everyone, accountable for doing what you all agreed upon.

If you do that, you'll Skyrocket. Happy coaching!

SKYROCKET PARTNER COACHING SERVICES

Michael Cary Sonbert and Skyrocket are available to provide the following services for interested partners:

Instructional Coaching Bootcamp

School Leader Bootcamp

Onsite School Leader Coaching

The Skyrocket School Leader Academy

School Diagnostics

Virtual Coaching

Teacher Training

Special Education Coaching

Diversity, Equity, and Inclusion Training

Keynotes

Please contact Michael for questions, feedback, and costs.
MichaelSonbert@WeWillSkyrocket.com

ABOUT THE AUTHOR

Michael Sonbert is the founder of Skyrocket Educator Training, which specializes in school leader and teacher training. Michael has personally trained leaders and teachers from over 80 cities around the world, and his Skyrocket frameworks are being used in hundreds of schools nationally. Before he started Skyrocket, Michael was a teacher, instructional coach, and the director of strategic partnerships at Mastery Charter Schools in Philadelphia. In his spare time, Michael is an autism advocate, a fiction writer, and the lead singer of the bands the Never Enders and Disco Thieves. He lives in New York with his wife and three children.

ACKNOWLEDGMENTS

This book only exists because of the generosity, humility, and brilliance of every educator who has allowed me the opportunity to learn from them. From the veterans who trained and coached me early on, to the leaders and teachers who welcome me into their schools, classrooms, and debriefs, to every school leader, teacher, teacher's assistant, and staff member in between who has sent an email, been gracious with their time, shown me hospitality in their schools and cities, provided me valuable feedback, or shared a smile, I am and continue to be forever grateful.

If not for my amazing wife, Gina, who lifts me up, inspires me, edits my work, and most magnanimously gives me permission to travel around the country while she takes care of our three children under six years old, I'd just be a person with some cool ideas and not much more. Gina, you are amazing. Thank you!

Thanks to Aqueelah Ellzy for taking a chance on a tattooed goon from Long Island when it would've been so easy not to.

Thanks to Mike Hammond for teaching me to be goal oriented, data focused, and intentional with my words and actions. I learned so much from you, both what you taught me explicitly and what I learned just from watching you lead our team. You had a perfect answer to every question I ever heard anyone ask you. I'm still striving for that.

Thanks to the team, both past and present, at Thomas High School in South Philly for all you taught me. Special shout-outs to Jill Dunchick, Kristy Fruit, Debi Durso, Jenny Smith, Lila Clark, and my mentor, Shannon Patterson.

Thanks to the Mastery Charter Schools' Instructional Coaching Team.

I think we caught lightning in a bottle back then. I miss your smarts, your pushes, and our happy hours. I think of each of you often.

Thanks to Jeff Pestrak, who, when told I had a lot of tattoos, including one on my neck, asked two questions after it was suggested Mastery hire me. First, "Can he teach?" Second, "Is the tattoo a swastika?" And after hearing "Yes," and "No," in that order, he said, "Hire him."

Thanks to Lindsey Alexander and Sal Borriello from Reading List Editorial. You made this book look amazing in every way. I can be a major pain in the ass. Thanks for not making me feel like one.

To Starr Sackstein for making this awesome introduction and for the guidance you provided along the way.

To Chris Webel and the team at the NIKE Work-Based Learning Center for letting me turn your school into a fashion shoot.

Thanks to Dave and Shelley Burgess for believing in this book and bringing it to the light of day. I am *so appreciative* of this opportunity.

To Matt Troha. I learn something from you every time we connect. Let's keep that going. One hundred hammers, my friend.

To Scott Gordon for your warmth when I arrived and your generosity when I left. I appreciate you more than you know.

To every last student and family I've had the opportunity to serve in some way. I thank you for your trust, your honesty, and your feedback. And to my former students, always remember, "Cool Breeze."

To Stacey and Dad. Thanks for always supporting me and my crazy dreams. I bet Mom is proud that I followed her lead and went into education. I bet she's proud of all of us. I love you both.

Thanks to Maryanne and Matty D (especially Maryanne!) for always being there for us while we're on this incredible journey. I hope the guest bed isn't too hard. But Matty, I bet it's nothing a twelve-year-old scotch can't fix.

Finally, *thank you* Jackie Kasher for seeing something in me that I didn't know was there. I love you, cuz.

And if I forgot you, I'll get you in the next one. I promise.

MORE FROM

Dave Burgess Consulting, Inc.

Since 2012, DBCI has been publishing books that inspire and equip educators to be their best. For more information on our titles or to purchase bulk orders for your school, district, or book study, visit DaveBurgessConsulting.com/DBCIbooks.

More Leadership & School Culture

Culturize by Jimmy Casas
Escaping the School Leader's Dunk Tank by Rebecca Coda and Rick Jetter
From Teacher to Leader by Starr Sackstein
The Innovator's Mind-set by George Couros
It's OK to Say They by Christy Whittlesey
Kids Deserve It! by Todd Nesloney and Adam Welcome
Let Them Speak by Rebecca Coda and Rick Jetter
The Limitless School by Abe Hege and Adam Dovico
The Pepper Effect by Sean Gaillard
The Principled Principal by Jeffrey Zoul and Anthony McConnell
Relentless by Hamish Brewer
The Secret Solution by Todd Whitaker, Sam Miller, and Ryan Donlan
Start. Right. Now. by Todd Whitaker, Jeffrey Zoul, and Jimmy Casas
Stop. Right. Now. by Jimmy Casas and Jeffrey Zoul
They Call Me "Mr. De" by Frank DeAngelis
Unmapped Potential by Julie Hasson and Missy Lennard
Word Shift by Joy Kirr
Your School Rocks by Ryan McLane and Eric Lowe

Like a PIRATE™ Series

Teach Like a PIRATE by Dave Burgess
eXPlore Like a Pirate by Michael Matera
Learn Like a Pirate by Paul Solarz
Play Like a Pirate by Quinn Rollins
Run Like a Pirate by Adam Welcome

Lead Like a PIRATE™ Series

Lead Like a PIRATE by Shelley Burgess and Beth Houf
Balance Like a Pirate by Jessica Cabeen, Jessica Johnson, and Sarah Johnson
Lead beyond Your Title by Nili Bartley
Lead with Culture by Jay Billy
Lead with Literacy by Mandy Ellis

Technology & Tools

50 Things You Can Do with Google Classroom by Alice Keeler and Libbi Miller
50 Things to Go Further with Google Classroom by Alice Keeler and Libbi Miller
140 Twitter Tips for Educators by Brad Currie, Billy Krakower, and Scott Rocco
Block Breaker by Brian Aspinall
Code Breaker by Brian Aspinall
Google Apps for Littles by Christine Pinto and Alice Keeler
Master the Media by Julie Smith
Reality Bytes by Christine Lion-Bailey, Jesse Lubinsky, and Micah Shippee
Shake Up Learning by Kasey Bell
Social LEADia by Jennifer Casa-Todd
Teaching Math with Google Apps by Alice Keeler and Diana Herrington
Teachingland by Amanda Fox and Mary Ellen Weeks

Teaching Methods & Materials

All 4s and 5s by Andrew Sharos
The Classroom Chef by John Stevens and Matt Vaudrey
Ditch That Homework by Matt Miller and Alice Keeler
Ditch That Textbook by Matt Miller
Don't Ditch That Tech by Matt Miller, Nate Ridgway, and Angelia Ridgway
EDrenaline Rush by John Meehan
Educated by Design by Michael Cohen, The Tech Rabbi
The EduProtocol Field Guide by Marlena Hebern and Jon Corippo
The EduProtocol Field Guide: Book 2 by Marlena Hebern and Jon Corippo
Instant Relevance by Denis Sheeran
LAUNCH by John Spencer and A.J. Juliani
Make Learning MAGICAL by Tisha Richmond
Pure Genius by Don Wettrick
The Revolution by Darren Ellwein and Derek McCoy
Shift This! by Joy Kirr

Spark Learning by Ramsey Musallam
Sparks in the Dark by Travis Crowder and Todd Nesloney
Table Talk Math by John Stevens
The Wild Card by Hope and Wade King
The Writing on the Classroom Wall by Steve Wyborney

Inspiration, Professional Growth & Personal Development
Be REAL by Tara Martin
Be the One for Kids by Ryan Sheehy
Creatively Productive by Lisa Johnson
The EduNinja Mind-set by Jennifer Burdis
Empower Our Girls by Lynmara Colón and Adam Welcome
The Four O'Clock Faculty by Rich Czyz
How Much Water Do We Have? by Pete and Kris Nunweiler
P Is for Pirate by Dave and Shelley Burgess
A Passion for Kindness by Tamara Letter
The Path to Serendipity by Allyson Apsey
Sanctuaries by Dan Tricarico
Shattering the Perfect Teacher Myth by Aaron Hogan
Stories from Webb by Todd Nesloney
Talk to Me by Kim Bearden
Teach Me, Teacher by Jacob Chastain
TeamMakers by Laura Robb and Evan Robb
Through the Lens of Serendipity by Allyson Apsey
The Zen Teacher by Dan Tricarico

Children's Books
Beyond Us by Aaron Polansky
Cannonball In by Tara Martin
Dolphins in Trees by Aaron Polansky
I Want to Be a Lot by Ashley Savage
The Princes of Serendip by Allyson Apsey
The Wild Card Kids by Hope and Wade King
Zom-Be a Design Thinker by Amanda Fox